The Egyptian Coffeehouse

The Egyptian Coffeehouse

Culture, Politics and Urban Space

Dalia Said Mostafa and Amina Elbendary

I.B. TAURIS
LONDON • NEW YORK • OXFORD • NEW DELHI • SYDNEY

I.B. TAURIS
Bloomsbury Publishing Plc
50 Bedford Square, London, WC1B 3DP, UK
1385 Broadway, New York, NY 10018, USA
29 Earlsfort Terrace, Dublin 2, Ireland

BLOOMSBURY, I.B. TAURIS and the I.B. Tauris logo are trademarks of
Bloomsbury Publishing Plc

First published in Great Britain 2021
This paperback edition published in 2022

Cover design: Adriana Brioso
Cover image © Photographer Adel Wassily

A catalogue record for this book is available from the British Library.

A catalog record for this book is available from the Library of Congress.

ISBN: HB: 978-0-7556-3524-5
PB: 978-0-7556-3549-8
ePDF: 978-0-7556-3529-0
eBook: 978-0-7556-3528-3

Typeset by Newgen KnowledgeWorks Pvt. Ltd., Chennai, India

To find out more about our authors and books visit www.bloomsbury.com
and sign up for our newsletters.

Contents

Illustrations

Figures

Plates

Acknowledgements

Our heartfelt thanks and gratitude go to our friend and colleague Dr Solava Ibrahim (Anglia Ruskin University) who embarked with us from the start on this book project and contributed to the structure and key ideas which have been developed in the book. Solava could not continue this journey with us to the end because she went on maternity leave.

Special and sincere thanks also go to our friend and colleague Dr Michelle Obeid (University of Manchester) who was the first to advise us on including a photo-story and contributed some extremely useful ideas on the structure of Chapter 7.

The support, appreciation and love of our families and friends over the past few years while working on the book made our writing journey enjoyable and pleasant: A big Thank You for the insurmountable love and care you have given us.

Special thanks are also due to photographer Adel Wassily whose pictures, specifically compiled for this book, have added an extra layer of value to the narrative.

Lastly, we are sincerely grateful to our interviewees in Cairo who agreed to contribute their time and wonderful stories about their favourite coffeehouses. Your passion for the Egyptian coffeehouses has been a true inspiration for us.

1

The Egyptian coffeehouse and urban space

Introduction

A place for socialization and entertainment, the coffeehouse has long been associated with popular communal gatherings in both urban and rural Egypt. The coffeehouse is a social space which was created and shaped over the decades by the people themselves in their neighbourhoods, and on the cities' squares and streets. It is a microcosm of the larger Egyptian society with its history of multiculturalism and great diversity. In a sense, the Egyptian coffeehouse subverts archaic forms of institutionalization and social exclusion. Hence, it has occupied in the popular imagination a sphere that is replete with new ideas, stories, memories and social networks. It is no surprise then that representations of the coffeehouse have taken countless forms in Egyptian literary works, films, songs, photographs, radio and television programmes and drama shows. Historically, the coffeehouse has also played a key role in political mobilization, as well as being a place where the unemployed could access job opportunities through meeting potential employers. Despite the coffeehouse's cultural centrality and sociopolitical importance in Egypt, academic research and publications on its significance remain sparse.

This volume aims to fill this academic gap through analysing, for the first time in a full study in English, the importance of the coffeehouse as an urban phenomenon which has cultural, historical, economic and political implications in the contemporary Egyptian society especially in the aftermath of the 25 January 2011 revolution. The main objectives of the volume can be summarized as follows: to theorize and unpack the role and influence of the coffeehouse as a significant feature of contemporary Egyptian life and social relationships; to illustrate the ways in which the coffeehouse has been depicted in the Egyptian cultural field, particularly in literature, cinema and song; to study the political, spatial and economic dynamics of the coffeehouse as an integral public space in the life of Egyptians; to demonstrate through highlighting specific examples of traditional coffeehouses in Cairo and Alexandria the various roles they play in these cities; and finally to offer some indicative public views of the coffeehouse's role through open-ended interviews with six residents of Cairo.

In Egypt, there are two widespread types of the coffeehouse (or *ahwa* as pronounced in the Egyptian vernacular): the first is the *ahwa baladi* (the traditional café/coffeeshop) which is found in almost every neighbourhood across the country and usually dominated by men's presence. The second type is the historical-cultural coffeehouse such as al-Fishawi in al-Hussein area in Islamic Cairo or the Naguib Mahfouz coffeehouse also in al-Hussein; or the well-known Café Riche on Talaat Harb Street in downtown Cairo; or al-Horriyya coffeehouse in Bab al-Louq (off Tahrir Square); or the multiple European-style coffeehouses in Alexandria's downtown Raml area (e.g. Trianon, Delice and Elite). This latter type of the historical-cultural coffeehouse is open for both men and women of different backgrounds and age groups. The contrast in the history and architecture of coffeehouses such as al-Fishawi, on the one hand, and Café Riche on the other, cannot be more fascinating as an indicator of the richness of the multifaceted architectural history of Egyptian cities. While al-Fishawi is immersed in Islamic Cairo (the old city) with its notable *bazaar* culture and spiritual ambience, Café Riche was founded in the early years of the twentieth century during the colonial era in the modern quarter of khedival Cairo (the new city), inspired by European architecture. The photographs which are included in this volume display some of these historical and architectural differences which are perceived in themselves as key signifiers of cosmopolitan culture in Egypt.

Indeed, the Egyptian coffeehouse best captures Henri Lefebvre's notion of 'social space'. In his seminal work *The Production of Space*, Lefebvre argues that social space is 'what permits fresh actions to occur, while suggesting others and prohibiting yet others. ... Social space implies a great diversity of knowledge.'[1] Social space also embodies political acts. Lefebvre explains that when we discuss *space* we must also consider what or who occupies this space, interrelationships and the activities that take place within it during a timeframe. For him, space considered in isolation of 'time' and 'energy' resembles 'an empty abstraction'.[2] Furthermore, David Harvey has remarked that 'what we do as well as what we understand is integrally dependent upon the primary spatio-temporal frame within which we situate ourselves'.[3] He states that in Lefebvre's work, urbanisation and the production of space are interlinked.[4] He adds: 'Particularly through the events of 1968, Lefebvre came to recognise the significance of urban conditions of daily life (as opposed to narrow concentration on work-place politics) as central in the evolution of revolutionary sentiments and politics'.[5] In this context, the Egyptian coffeehouse can be seen as a space where social relations are produced and developed over periods of time; hence this space plays a crucial role in formulating such concepts as *identity* and *affect*, and indeed has the potential to serve in mobilizing for political and social movements as the following chapters will demonstrate. According to Lefebvre, 'Groups, classes or factions of classes cannot constitute themselves, or recognize one another, as "subjects" unless they generate (or produce) a space'.[6]

Since the turn of the twenty-first century, there has been an increasing proliferation in Egyptian cities, particularly in middle- and upper-class suburbs, of famous global coffeeshop chains such as Starbucks and Costa, and other local chains/brands such as Cilantro and Beano's that emulate the global ones. These act as markers of class and distinguish their customers and social ambience from those of both the *ahwa baladi* (traditional café) and the historical-cultural coffeehouses. These new coffeeshop chains are more popular among the younger population and can also be found in large shopping malls and five-star hotels.[7] Needless to say, some people frequent different coffeeshops on various occasions, possibly having more than one favourite type of café space. In this volume, the focus will be on two types of coffeehouses: the traditional *ahwa* (or café/coffeeshop); and the historical-cultural coffeehouse, as opposed to the Westernized/modern chains of coffeeshops. Yet, we will draw some comparisons between the traditional coffeehouses and the modern coffeeshops in order to explore ideas related to gender and class dynamics. The reader will also find informed reflections on these different café cultures, particularly in regard to the traditional *ahwa*, through the testimonies of our interviewees in Chapter 7.

Spending time at the coffeehouse is an everyday Egyptian social practice which sheds light on notions of belonging and identity formations, as well as gender and class relations. This practice also illuminates our understanding of Egyptian city life. As David Harvey has argued (based on his reading of the sociologist Robert Park's work), 'the kind of cities we want to live in cannot be divorced from what kind of people we want to be or what kind of humanity we want to create.'[8] We build the kind of cities we want to live in, and in turn cities shape our collective identity. One characteristic which defines the Egyptian urban space is the *ahwa baladi*, hence it has occupied a signifying dimension in the popular imagination. It is a place which encompasses many things simultaneously: socialization, entertainment, a support network, consolidation of friendships, in addition to being a place for cultural debates and political mobilization. On the other hand, it has a 'sinister' aspect that is widely known among customers: informers and spies who work for the police and security apparatus also inhabit the coffeehouse so as to report on dissenting political activists and opposition figures.

Choosing the type of coffeehouse to frequent can be an indicator of gender dynamics. Mark Allen Peterson provides an interesting discussion about traditional and Westernized cafés in different areas in Cairo, particularly those which cater for middle- and upper-class customers. As he remarks, 'Coffee houses of different kinds are sites of gender performance, places where particular kinds of masculinity and femininity are constructed.'[9] This can be seen clearly when visiting a traditional *ahwa baladi* in a popular suburb in an Egyptian city where we find it inhabited mainly by men smoking shisha, in a striking contrast to the modern coffeeshops such as Cilantro or Retro where women feel at ease mingling with friends or even spending time on their own. Peterson describes these modern coffeeshops as 'translocal places' where one is able to 'construct a cosmopolitan identity'.[10] He defines this state as 'being able to afford entry into such a space and by being comfortable in it – that is, knowing one's place in the world'.[11]

Peterson also expands the discussion on how groups of men, even from the upper classes, gather in the *ahwa baladi* to assert their masculine attitudes and behaviours, whereas they feel reluctant to do so in the modern coffeeshops while in the company of female friends. Through various interviews and conversations with male friends, Peterson concludes that Cairene coffeehouses and coffeeshops are important sites to observe and understand gender and class relations. Yet, we can add here that some of these characteristics described by

Peterson have remarkably changed in opening the traditional *ahwa baladi* to female customers in the aftermath of the 2011 Egyptian revolution, particularly in Cairo's downtown area around Tahrir Square.

In the following chapters, we will analyse the significant ways in which these gendered identities are represented in a selection of literary and cinematic works, especially how women can be seen in some films owning and managing coffeehouses and traditional cafés in both popular and middle-class neighbourhoods. We also aim to shed light on several artistic works produced in recent years which point to a renewed interest in the theme of 'coffee' and 'coffeehouse'.

In addition to the large repertoire of representations which permeate Egyptian films of the *ahwa baladi*, we have been able to depict a number of songs which were produced post-2011 and have addressed the 'coffeehouse' as a main theme. These include Islam Ali's song 'Qahwa baladi';[12] and Haidy's song 'Ahwa baladi',[13] which is a play on the Arabic verb 'ahwa' (I love).[14] The well-known singer Hamza Namira also performed a song entitled '3alahwa' (At the café) for the radio channel *Nogoum FM*.[15] Moreover, an initiative entitled 'El qahwa baladi' began in Port Sa'id city in 2013 by a group of artists who aimed to revive the role of the coffeehouse in Egyptian cultural life by organizing a variety of performances, poetry readings and cultural debates at the city's coffeehouses.[16] It is also interesting to note that BBC Radio 3 broadcasted a programme entitled 'Stirring up a revolution' by Tarek Osman in June 2013.[17] In it, Osman interviews a number of artists and writers, most notably the veteran novelist Ibrahim Abdel Meguid, and discusses with them the prominence of the coffeehouse in Egyptian cultural life. Furthermore, during the first year of the 2011 revolution, a group of friends started an initiative entitled 'There is no shame in work', where each of them worked for one day in a profession they never did before, one of these was to be a *qahwagi* (tea/coffee maker) at a traditional café in the city.[18]

The neoliberal city's *ahawi* (cafés) and limitations of public space

In attempting to situate the expansion of outdoor *ahawi* (cafés – vernacular Egyptian plural for *ahwa*) in Cairo and other large Egyptian cities such as

Alexandria and Port Saʿid, it is key to engage what scholar Asef Bayat refers to as 'the city-inside-out'.[19] Bayat suggests that neoliberal economic policies in countries like Egypt and the larger MENA region have led to significant spatial implications for the 'subaltern' population in urban centres in particular. He proposes the following:

> A key spatial feature of the neoliberal city relates to double and dialectical processes of 'inside-outing' and 'enclosure'. In the first place, the neoliberal city is a 'city-inside-out', where a massive number of urban residents, the subaltern, become compelled to operate, subsist, or simply live on the public spaces—in the streets, in a substantial 'out-doors economy'.[20]

By 'enclosure' as opposed to 'inside-outing', Bayat means the ways in which middle- and upper classes move away from the crowded city centres to the outskirts to establish private compounds and gated communities. Thus, we argue that in response to the increasing unemployment in the urban centres in Egypt, opening new outdoor traditional cafés (or *ahawi baladi*) is part of the expansion of the informal sector and casual work. These *ahawi* can be opened anywhere in Egyptian cities, for example, on side streets, in small alleyways, in slum areas and even in courtyards between buildings. It is in the presence of the outdoor cafés, among other phenomena, that we can literally and metaphorically foreground this concept proposed by Bayat: the city is inside out.

Bayat also points out that this informal sector of survival is no longer the domain of the poor, but 'informal life', as he remarks, has 'become a facet of educated middle class existence', while explaining that many public sector employees have resorted to second and third jobs in the 'out-door economy' to compensate for their low income. Hence, Bayat suggests: 'In today's neoliberal cities, out-door economies and public presence are necessities and (for some women) spaces for self-expression.'[21]

The informal economy in Egypt has grown exponentially as a result of neoliberal economic policies since the 1970s (e.g. see Bayat 1997; Deboulet 2009; El-Mahdi and Marfleet 2009; Ismail 2011; Abdelrahman 2014, 2016). In David Sims's seminal book *Understanding Cairo: The Logic of a City out of Control*, the author provides a powerful case to demonstrate how the informal sector in a megacity like Cairo has in fact made it function relatively well and has maintained its core. As he remarks,

Cairo has generated its own logics of accommodation and development, and … these operate largely outside the truncated powers of government or are at best in a symbiotic relation with its weakness. For lack of a better word, these logics can be called 'informal'.[22]

We argue here that part of understanding the urban dynamics within the Egyptian cities' informal sector is to consider the opening of small outdoor *ahawi* (cafés) which cater for low-income customers, many of whom work in the informal economy such as street vendors, construction workers, mechanics, drivers, messengers and others. The outdoor *ahawi* provide them with a 'second space' (after home) for socialization and for job search in contrast to what some scholars have described as a 'third space' (after home and the work place) in reference to the modern European coffeeshops.[23] Traditionally in Egypt, different professions also have had their *ahwa* hangouts. For example, *ahwet al-tabbakhin* (The Cooks' Café) was where out-of-work cooks would go to meet but also to look for job opportunities through their acquaintances. Employers would usually go there to look for new employees. This brief example (which is also supported by views of our interviewees) shows how the *ahwa baladi* is perceived as a key place within the informal economy sector where the unemployed can potentially find work.

Asef Bayat expands his ideas about the city-inside-out saying that this is not limited to spatial features of working life, but it resonates even more powerfully in 'everyday lifeworlds'.[24] In response to the small and stifling narrow living spaces in popular and slum areas in Egypt, for example, people stretch their existence outdoors. Bayat further explains that by bringing their social activities to the streets, the 'informal subaltern' are engaged in what he refers to as 'street politics'. He makes this remark:

Streets may actually serve as an indispensable asset/capital for them to subsist and reproduce economic as well as cultural life. In both of these arenas, the actors are involved in a relation of power over the control of public space and public order. They are involved, in other words, in street politics. Street politics, then, describes a set of conflicts and the attendant implications between certain groups or individuals and the authorities, which are shaped and expressed in the physical and social space of streets – from back alleys to the main avenues, from invisible city escapes to main squares.[25]

One can argue that this observation captures with precision what we saw happening with the breakout of the January 2011 revolution in Egypt, when masses of people from all walks of life sprang from the 'back alleys' and 'invisible city escapes' to the main streets and squares to claim and occupy them. Moreover, as Bayat illustrates, 'streets are not just places where conflicts are shaped and/or expressed. They are also venues where people forge collective identities and extend their solidarities beyond their immediate familiar circles to include also the unknown, the strangers.'[26] Because the traditional coffeehouse opens onto the Egyptian streets, we argue, it is one key public place where these collective identities are shaped and consolidated. Bayat goes on to say that this stretching out onto public space enables the urban poor to 'become a party in the contest over shaping the urban form, and molding the urban texture, the domains of the social, the cultural, and the sensory: noise, smell, and sight.'[27] The coffeehouses, or tea-houses as Bayat refers to them, become one of these entertainment or socialization places, particularly for the unemployed youth and the pensioners who can afford their prices as they spend hours there to pass the time. As Bayat concludes:

> In the city-inside-out, the subaltern are seen and felt to be almost everywhere. In fact they are everywhere. As carriers of a certain habitus – mode of being, behaving, and doing things – the poor are present in the main streets, public parks, and alleyways; in buses, tea houses, hang-out squares, and on the side-walks. … [T]hrough their overwhelming presence in the public arenas with their overpowering physique, looks, gaze, behavior and through their life-style, noise, and smell, the subaltern unintentionally compel the disgruntled elites to retreat into their own safe havens.[28]

Bayat describes the agency of the subaltern to assert their rights to public space as 'the art of presence'. He explains this idea, saying:

> This art of presence signifies the ability to assert collective will in spite of all odds, to circumvent the constraints, utilizing what is possible, and discover new spaces within which to make oneself heard, seen, felt, and realized. The art of presence serves as the medium through which the subaltern may achieve survival by *repossession* as a response to their status of *dispossession* in the neoliberal city. And the city-inside-out becomes the spatial expression of subaltern politics in the current neoliberal urbanity.[29]

Bayat's theoretical premises about informal economies and the presence of the subaltern on the streets of the neoliberal city, the contestation over public space and the production of outdoor economies inform to a great extent our analysis of the centrality of the coffeehouse in contemporary Egyptian cultural, social and urban life. The coffeehouse is part of this contested public space. Whenever we pass by a traditional *ahwa* in Egypt, we usually find it full of people, immersed in various activities: playing backgammon, cards and dominoes or PlayStation; smoking shisha; having a variety of Egyptian-style hot drinks; watching football; watching news, speeches or talk shows; or simply chitting and chatting. For Egyptians, the café culture is associated with loud voices, music and football matches; with noise. Its noise mingles with other distinct sounds of the city: traffic, the voices and laughter of groups of passers-by, street vendors calling around to sell their merchandise, and much more. The café is central to the renewal of everyday urban living. In fact, the Egyptian coffeehouse is a treasure box of ideas, stories, memories, song, dance and endless social networks, as the following chapters aim to illustrate.

The Egyptian coffeehouse in the popular imagination

Perhaps it was writer Naguib Mahfouz more than any other Egyptian novelist who brought to our attention the cultural and political significance of the coffeehouse through his novels as well as his own lifestyle. The coffeehouse was like Mahfouz's 'second home' where he spent much of his time meeting with acquaintances and readers, delivering public talks and discussing literary matters. The walls of Café Riche are witness to this where we find a large picture in black and white of Mahfouz hung in the centre surrounded by other pictures of iconic literary figures. It was to a large degree the Mahfouzian novel which situated the coffeehouse as key to the city's modernity, as a place larger than life where in some novels the coffeehouse gives character to the city and indeed shapes its spatial elements. These themes will be explored in Chapter 4 of this book.

In his reflections in *Cairo from Edge to Edge*, the prolific Egyptian novelist Sonallah Ibrahim captures the cultural significance of Café Riche, precisely because it was home to Mahfouz and his friends for many years, saying:

> The natural way for any writer to begin the day is to grab a pen and paper or to sit at the computer – if, like myself, he is very modern. But many Cairene writers prefer a more pragmatic beginning, capable of uplifting the creative powers: Tahrir Square is their point of departure. ... For one thing, the importance of the square lies in the fact that it leads, just a few metres from the underground Metro station, to the café where the Nobel writer Naguib Mahfouz was accustomed to sit, every morning, to read the papers and have coffee.[30]

Ibrahim goes on to point to the historical value of Café Riche (which was opened in 1908) and describes its 'golden age' in the 1960s and 1970s 'when it used to bustle with the most vital literary debates',[31] and groups sitting around its tables discussing new fiction, journals, film scripts, plays, while smoking and drinking beer. But this vibrant intellectual atmosphere also had a sinister side to it as Ibrahim reminds us, 'when many were taken to detention camps or prisons because of a word or a joke recorded in a secret report, written at a neighbouring table'.[32] Thus, in the popular imagination, Egyptians have known coffeehouses to embody these two striking and contrasting aspects: a place for entertainment, socialization, intellectual debates and political mobilization on one hand; and on the other, a place where spies and *mukhbireen* (informers) for the police and the state security apparatus are present to watch and record any political dissidence against the regime.

Interestingly, in an article published on the website of the University of Pennsylvania on 19 June 2017,[33] Jacquie Posey reports on one of the university's PhD students, Alon Tam, who is investigating the history of the Cairo coffeehouses in the nineteenth and early part of the twentieth centuries as public and political places which Egyptian and British spies often frequented to get information about nationalist and anti-regime political mobilization. Tam has discovered new material in the British National Archives and other archives in the United Kingdom and France about Egyptian and British spy reports which will certainly shed new light on the political history of Cairo's coffeehouses. Tam's dissertation also investigates how the coffeehouses during that period were 'hubs for revolutionaries who met to organize demonstrations and plan protests'.[34] This line of research, which focuses on a specific historical period, highlights the fact that Egyptian coffeehouses are increasingly drawing the attention of researchers which promises to expand future contributions in this subject area.

Thus, the coffeehouse in the Egyptian context has deeply rooted historical, cultural, economic and political implications which are ingrained in the popular imagination, and is to a large extent a signifier of the social diversity found in the country. The coffeehouse is a popular invention par excellence, and hence it combines paradoxical elements, progressive and regressive: it is an open space where any passer-by can step in; but it can also be a space where informers and spies disguise themselves to report on political dissidents. It is a place which has the potential to be free of social constraints; but it can also turn into one where women, for example, might be harassed or their presence rejected.

The *ahawi* (cafés) during and after January 2011

A number of scholars have drawn attention to the impact of the 25 January 2011 revolution on the reshaping and reorganization of public space in various Egyptian cities, especially Cairo, home to the iconic Tahrir Square (Mehrez 2012; Mitchell 2012; Nagati and Stryker 2013; Abaza 2013, 2014 among others). As having been on Tahrir Square ourselves during the first 18 days of the revolution, we witnessed first-hand how all the shops were closed around the downtown area, except for very few *ahawi*. The revolutionaries would take a break during those early days and gather at El Borsa, Zahrat al-Bustan or al-Nadwa al-Thaqafiyya cafés. It was phenomenal to see how these cafés transformed into hubs for political discussions, heated debates and plans upon plans for what to do next. The whole area around Tahrir was pulsing with people, their dreams and their stories about a better future for themselves and for the nation.

As the activists and revolutionaries on Tahrir Square and its surrounding area continued to draw a new spatial map of downtown Cairo, the outdoor *ahawi* became part of this new urban scene. The visibility on the streets of the protestors with their vast diversity in social class, education, gender and age continued in the aftermath of the revolution for at least three years until the authorities started to close down some of these cafés. For example, El Borsa café no longer exists. Even the historical and iconic Groppi coffeehouse on Talaat Harb Square has been closed down 'for renovations' for a number of years. In this context, we argue that spatial relations and the intervention to reconfigure public space, whether by collective groups of people or by the authorities, are key to our efforts in unlocking the debates around the 2011 revolution and its aftermath.

Over the past nine years, a large volume of interdisciplinary academic work has emerged on the 2011 Arab revolutions and uprisings (or the 'Arab Spring') to explore their remarkable impact on spatial and cultural transformations in urban settings in particular: the agency and power of the people to reclaim the streets and squares of their cities; visual and popular culture; the documentary versus the fictional in film, literature, song and so on. This new body of work helps us to situate the diverse roles of coffeehouses on urban streets, in neighbourhoods and in small alleys in Egyptian cities.

In her article 'Bodies in Alliance and the Politics of the Street', Judith Butler describes the significance of the collective organization of 'bodies' on the streets during the 2011 Arab uprisings. She makes this key observation:

> And when crowds move outside the square, to the side street or the back alley, to the neighborhoods where streets are not yet paved, then something more happens. At such a moment, politics is no longer defined as the exclusive business of public sphere distinct from a private one, but it crosses that line again and again, bringing attention to the way that politics is already in the home, or on the street, or in the neighborhood, or indeed in those virtual spaces that are unbound by the architecture of the public square.[35]

Butler's remark intersects with Charles Tripp's illuminating ideas in his book *The Power and the People: Paths of Resistance in the Middle East*. Tripp argues that one of the most important features of the Arab uprisings in 2011 was the contestation over public space and its occupation. This was the way that the people were able to make their physical presence felt and to demand recognition for their rights.[36] This kind of 'disorderly' behaviour challenges, and in many ways, subverts the state's attempts to make public space orderly, neat and free of uncontrolled behaviour, according to Tripp.[37] The state wants to show that the people respect its authority, its public institutions and power as for them, maintaining an orderly public space is a matter of life or death, that is life or death of its grip on power, as Tripp argues.[38] He further observes that the importance of public space lies in the fact that it is where the state shows its public face; where it presents 'an edifice of seemingly solid material weight'.[39] Tripp goes on to make this crucial remark:

> Public defiance in turn mobilises growing numbers of people, giving them a shared language in which to voice their grievances and providing a framework for action that can change the balance of power itself. It is for this very reason, that across the region, political authorities have responded with ferocious violence against open forms of public defiance and resistance.[40]

Perhaps this is why the first step that the Supreme Council of the Armed Forces (SCAF) took on 11 February 2011 when Omar Soliman announced the stepping down of ex-president Hosni Mubarak was to ensure that all squares and streets around the country were cleared from the protestors. Since that day, the tug of war started between the state (and its tools of power: police, army, and intelligence apparatus) and the dissenting political activists. During this process over the past few years of reasserting control and power on the streets, the dynamics of accessing and using public space and along with it the identity of Egyptian squares and streets have significantly changed.

From our perspective as citizens, streets, squares and parks are defined as public space but the state deploys its police force to guard them. The citizens feel that they are under surveillance in this seemingly free public sphere. Thus, as Charles Tripp argues, these sites are precisely the areas where the people confront the state authorities. He adds that streets, squares and parks also provide two key features of resistance against the official narrative of the state: space and numbers.[41] On the one hand, people want to uphold their right to public space; and on the other, the state aims to maintain its power and authority over this space. Tripp argues that it is precisely at this point of openness intersecting with restriction and limitation that resistance against state authority emerges. As he puts it: 'It is both a statement of physical presence and a demand for recognition of rights.'[42] Indeed, public space can become a double-edged sword: subverting state control at one end of the scale, or reinforcing its authority at the other end. Since 2011, we have seen these two patterns with different degrees of intensity happening so forcefully on the streets and squares of public domain in Egypt.

In the light of the above discussion, it is one of our objectives in the following chapters to examine the evolving spatial connotation of *ahawi* on the streets. There is a distinct political symbolism embedded in the act of placing tables and chairs outdoors for large numbers of customers (constantly seen, heard and felt) as possibly one way of reinforcing the presence of the people and making them visible in large numbers on a daily basis on the streets.

This book

The book aims to introduce the reader to a key feature of Egyptian urban living, the traditional and cultural coffeehouses. Our objective is to map out the historical roots of the coffeehouse and also to study its cultural, spatial, economic and political implications in a diverse range of works by Egyptian writers and artists. Chapter 2, 'Betwixt and between: The arrival of coffeeshops in Cairo as an urban phenomenon', tells the story of the emergence of coffee and coffeeshops in the early modern and modern periods in Egypt and the Middle East more broadly. The chapter highlights the influence of the coffee trade and the early coffeeshops in the Egyptian urban landscape, particularly Cairo, and the creation of a new in-between space that was both public and private. It also discusses the cultural effects of the rise of coffeeshops on literary and cultural production, paving the way for its crucial role in the twentieth century.

Chapters 3 and 4, 'Locating the *Ahwa* in the work of Egyptian writers' and 'The case of Naguib Mahfouz: Storyteller of the Egyptian coffeehouse', will look at a selection of representations of the coffeehouses in novels by Egyptian writers with a focus on the contributions of the Nobel laureate Naguib Mahfouz, whom the authors consider as *the literary chronicler* of the Egyptian coffeehouse. Chapter 3 analyses the attachment of writers to coffeehouses and how they have reflected this in their fictional works, such as the prominent novelist Gamal al-Ghitani. We also examine key literary texts which portray the symbiotic relationship between characters and coffeehouses such as Ibrahim Aslan's novel *The Heron* (1981), Mohammad al-Bisati's novella *The Glass*

Coffeehouse (1979) and Ahmed Mourad's novel *1919* (2014). Chapter 4 focuses on popular works by Naguib Mahfouz including *Midaq Alley* (1946), *Sugar Street* (1957), *Autumn Quail* (1962), *Karnak-Café* (1974) and *The Coffeehouse* (1988). In this way, these two chapters will show, through a fictional lens, how the coffeehouse is specifically intertwined with urban living, politics and modernity, as well as the history of particular locations, streets and alleys.

Chapter 5, 'Multilayered representations of the coffeehouse in Egyptian cinema', focuses on a selection of films (including some adaptations from Naguib Mahfouz's works) made in different periods to trace the cultural and spatial connotations of the coffeehouse in a multiplicity of visual representations. In fact, it would not be an exaggeration to argue that the *ahwa baladi* figures in a huge output of Egyptian films since the inception of cinema in the early part of the twentieth century, which is a superb indication of the centrality of this place in the life of Egyptians. As cinema is one of the most popular entertainment media in Egypt, and Egyptian films from different eras are shown on television as a daily staple, this chapter will highlight key signifiers of gender and class relationships through selected representations of the coffeehouse.

Chapter 6, 'Egyptian singers and performers: An integral relation to the coffeehouse', outlines a historical dimension to the Egyptian coffeehouses as entertainment places since the eighteenth century where popular singers and dancers used to perform, but we also expand the analysis into the twentieth century to explore a number of iconic songs in the popular imagination which revolve around the theme of coffee and coffeehouse. Moreover, the chapter demonstrates how the coffeehouse transformed into a *political site* in the experience of the Canal Zone cities, particularly Port Saʿid, where singers used to gather to compose patriotic lyrics and songs along with the melodies of their traditional instrument, *simsimiyya*, about resistance against the British colonialists and other invaders of their cities. Finally, the chapter engages with several cases where the theme of the traditional coffeehouse was revived by a number of younger singers in the aftermath of the 2011 revolution and the social and political implications of this revival.

Chapter 7, 'Pictures, voices and narratives of coffeehouses', provides a 'photo-story' displaying eleven photographs of iconic cafés and coffeehouses in Cairo and Alexandria compiled specifically for this volume by the Egyptian photographer Adel Wassily. Testimonies narrated by six interviewees from Cairo telling about their relation to and experience of coffeehouses aim to draw the reader into the specificities of this urban space of social, political, economic and cultural interaction while shedding much light on identity formations and national belonging in contemporary Egyptian society. Through this extended photo-story, we aim to demonstrate the vital role of the coffeehouse in shaping urban living, and in Egyptian city life more broadly. Furthermore, the narratives presented highlight the important debate about the impact of the changing spatial and economic dynamics of the coffeehouse in post-2011 society.

Finally, the 'Conclusion' will underscore the links between the oral narratives and the cultural history of coffeehouses, while reflecting on their continuing influence on the social life of Egyptians and suggesting new directions of research on this lively topic. Last but not least, we need to emphasize that although we acknowledge the vast popularity of representing the coffeehouse in Egyptian television drama series, we believe that such representations require a separate volume in its own right due to the enormous presence of café culture in drama.

2

Betwixt and between: The arrival of coffeeshops in Cairo as an urban phenomenon

Introduction: A historical overview of the emergence of coffee in the Middle East

A visitor to Cairo and to many Arab cities today would be hard-pressed to avoid the ubiquitous coffeeshops. One might be forgiven assuming that they have always been there: so traditional, almost timeless they seem, coffeeshops might appear to be inherent components of this elusive 'Islamic City'. But in fact, coffeeshops came in the late Middle Ages. They weren't always there. This chapter provides a broad historical context for the emergence of coffee as a drink in the Middle East and its arrival to Egypt along with the development of coffeeshops as distinct sites or spaces in between the public and the private that opened the doors for new types of interaction between people.

Coffeeshops, rather unsurprisingly, appeared with coffee. The earliest references to coffee suggest that it appeared, without much fanfare, as a drink in the Middle East in the second half of the fifteenth century. A century later, coffeeshops had spread and become an important feature at least of urban life. The coffeeshop provided Middle Eastern urban societies with a much-needed space for social and cultural interaction. This was especially the case for newly mobile urban middle classes who were eager to use this new semi-public space. And while some cultural and social practices were popular with the elites and their entourage before gaining a wider following, in the case of coffee and its culture the opposite was true. Coffee gained popularity first among the popular urban classes before spreading to higher levels of society.

Dating the spread of coffee in Cairo or other cities in the Middle East isn't very easy. Most historians refer to a crisis in the early sixteenth century as an indication of both the proliferation of the drink as well as some of the social and cultural practices surrounding it. The story goes that a Sufi (a Muslim mystic) – or Sufis – introduced the coffee drink from Ethiopia to Yemen and from Yemen to Mecca where it spread among other Sufis in the holy city. The link between the drink and Sufi men recurs in several sources and gives the drink a stamp of sanctity and acceptability. The drink made from coffee beans had the effects of alerting Sufis and helping them stay awake at night to perform their *dhikr* (remembrance of God) rituals. Since many of the members of Sufi *tariqas* (orders) by the Middle Ages were also craftsmen and tradesmen, and others were religious scholars by profession, they had day jobs, ones that could have been physically demanding as well. The coffee drink naturally alerted them, gave them a boost of energy as they embarked on their additional spiritual rituals and stave off sleep. As coffee reached Mecca, in the early sixteenth century, legend goes that the newly appointed *muhtasib* (market and public morals inspector) of the holy city, Khayr Bek, was alerted to the behaviour of Sufis who drank it outside or close to the Haram mosque at night.[1] That behaviour, people congregating at night around a drink, was suspicious enough to warrant a complaint.

When Khayr Bek inquired about the gathering he was told that it was to drink a substance that had become fashionable and was made of the husks of a plant brought in from Yemen. Furthermore, he was told that

> this drink had spread in Mecca, and had come to be sold in Mecca in places similar to taverns (*khammarat*), and that some people – men and women – got together over it with tambours (*duff*) and bowed stringed instruments (*rabab*) and other musical instruments, and that also congregating where it was sold were people who played chess and the *manqala* and other games played for money and other things forbidden by the sacred shari'a.[2]

This synopsis of what happened in coffeehouses, which contrasts with the image of Sufis drinking coffee to stay alert for *dhikr*, gives us a faint impression of the atmosphere that prevailed at least in some coffeehouses. The report was given to the newly appointed *muhtasib* at the end of the Mamluk period and is relayed by al-Jaziri in the context of suspicion of people gathered to drink coffee and criticism of the behaviour that had become popular: discursively it comes in a negative light in this text. However, it still reflects something perhaps of the behaviour in coffeehouses or of the possibilities they allowed: public places where people of different genders might potentially mingle freely and pass their time.

It is telling that both men and women are mentioned in this reference, as well as music and games. It is this liberty that was new to public space and that was deemed dangerous by some. It is difficult to gauge to what extent the presence of women was common in pre-modern coffeehouses though most indications suggest that it was not. At least 'respectable' women would not be seen hanging around this new social space. Except for a few references here and there that allude to the presence of female entertainers inside coffeehouses, or men dressed as women also performing inside coffeehouses, and usually in a derogatory or disapproving context, the coffeehouses of the early modern Middle East and of Cairo were masculine socialization sites. The true cause for the complaint and the *muhtasib*'s chagrin gives a reason for speculation; some reports indicate that he was upset because the coffee-drinkers also satirized him. A council of expert 'ulama and physicians was convened, a report sent to senior 'ulama in Cairo to demand a *fatwa* (religious legal opinion), and a debate ensued. We know through the later treatise of al-Jaziri (fl.1558) that eventually the consensus of the 'ulama was on the permissibility of the coffee drink. Al-Jaziri's treatise *'Umdat al-safwa fi hall al-qahwa* (The Noble's Guide to the Permissibility of Coffee) is the earliest source that describes the social and legal reception of coffee in the Arabic-speaking Middle East.

There were various legal reactions to coffee as it spread and became popular among people from different walks of life. The variation and discomfort of some is even reflected in the vocabulary used to refer to the drink: *qahwa*, the common word for the drink, is one of the words used to refer to wine. Derived from a root that refers to making something repugnant or lessening a desire, *qahwa* was used to refer to wine which lessens desire for food and then later for coffee which lessens desire for sleep.[3] The association carried some uncomfortable connotations. Some scholars called for banning the drink, while others argued that banning the dissolute behaviour associated with its drinking should not be extended to the drink itself.[4] That was to become the mainstream opinion. However, in the meantime, various ruling authorities banned its drinking in the mid-sixteenth century.[5] Although medieval sources refer to repeated bans on the consumption of coffee itself, history proves these were not to be long-lasting.[6]

The spread of coffee and coffeehouses in Cairo

Bans notwithstanding, by the time the Turkish traveller Mustafa 'Ali visited Cairo in 1599, he found remarkable 'the multitude of coffee-houses ..., the concentration of coffee-houses at every step, and of perfect places where people can assemble'.[7] By the first half of the nineteenth century, E. W. Lane would estimate that 'Cairo contains above a "thousand kahwehs" or coffee-shops'.[8]

Al-Jaziri also narrates that coffee first appeared in Cairo around al-Azhar and was introduced by the Yemenis living in the neighbourhood of the famous mosque around the turn of the sixteenth century.[9] It was the Sufis repeating *dhikr* who drank it on Monday and Friday nights in particular, and they were joined by common people who attended the *dhikr* sessions. Coffee was drunk and sold publicly in the neighbourhood of al-Azhar.[10] Another narrative also included in al-Jaziri's text refers to a woman who was selling the coffee drink in Mecca with her face uncovered, suggesting that there were itinerant sellers or peddlers of the drink, in addition to coffeehouses.[11] People were also very quickly drinking and serving it at home.[12] The repeated bans by officials usually did not last long as the public in cities like Mecca or Cairo soon went back not only to drinking it but also to operating coffeeshops.[13]

While coffee was eventually deemed a lawful drink by mainstream Muslim jurists, the coffeehouse on the other hand was subject to censure by religious scholars and vigilantes, and occasional bans by the authorities.[14] A distinction was created early on between the drink and the places where it was drunk.[15] Indeed, even in his treatise in defence of coffee, al-Jaziri alludes to some of the negative behaviour occasionally associated with its drinkers which he argued rulers should ban. Such behaviour included mixing coffee with intoxicants as well as indulging in gossip especially of a sexual nature, lies and rumours.[16] Hanging out to talk and exchange news, before the advent of mass media, was one of the popular pastimes associated with coffeehouses.[17] However, these places often had louche reputations where drug addicts and the riffraff would congregate, not respectable members of the middle class. This is reflected in Mustafa 'Ali's observations as early as the late sixteenth century: 'The coffee houses of Egypt are filled mostly with dissolute persons and opium-eaters.'[18] In a case from the court of Qanatir al-Siba' in Cairo in 1655, a court employee was reprimanded for spending time in coffeehouses.[19] As a respectable agent of the law, his association with the clientele of the coffeehouse and his informal behaviour there (he removed his turban and sat at ease) were damaging to his reputation. The censure serves at the same time to highlight how a relatively broad cross-section of early modern society frequented coffeeshops and could potentially cross paths.[20]

Thus began a continuing theme in the history of coffeeshops. They are popular and they are suspicious because they allow groups of people – mostly men – to congregate not always with a clear purpose, and to talk. Idle talk can be dangerous for the ruling authorities; it is money for the merchant.

Coffee and merchants

That coffee and coffeeshops became popular from the sixteenth century onwards is clear. Figuring out *why* is harder. The drink itself was an attraction but that is only part of the appeal. Indeed today, coffeeshops tend to serve more cups of tea than of coffee. But in the late Middle Ages people drank coffee in various settings. Most likely it was first popular with Sufis and the working classes, and then spread among the elite. The elite also drank coffee at their residences where it eventually acquired social etiquette of its own. But aside from the popularity of the drink, the space itself seems to have been attractive. In contrast to taverns, coffeeshops were places that respectable members of the community could easily patronise. Since Islamic law was relatively strict in regulating the consumption of alcohol by Muslims, taverns and drinking houses were at best tolerated as part of the shady marginal urban space but more often banned and routinely subject to attacks and censure by the authorities and vigilantes. Coffee, on the other hand, did not suffer the same stigma as alcohol. This made coffeeshops an attractive economic investment as well.

Research shows that coffee merchants played an important role in the proliferation and popularity of the drink and the institution. As scholars have argued, the crisis that occurred in the long-distance trade of pepper and spice by the penetration of Dutch and European merchants by the beginning of the seventeenth century created price fluctuations in the trade and prompted many Egyptian and Arab merchants of the Red Sea trade to direct major parts of their investments to the coffee trade instead, which was more stable.[21] Simultaneously, culinary tastes changed in Europe, and spices after becoming common place fell out of favour leading to a further decline in demand while coffee became the new fashionable consumable product.[22] Henceforth, coffee became an important commodity in the Red Sea trade. Unlike pepper which was procured from Asia and where Egyptian and Middle Eastern merchants were facing competition from the Dutch and European trading companies, coffee was brought from within the region, from Yemen, and was hence much more accessible, and its prices more stable.[23] Despite some misgivings about coffee and its public consumption, it soon spread to the elite. Not only were they increasingly frequenting coffeehouses and investing in the coffee trade, some also invested in coffeehouses. The seventeenth-century head of the merchants' guild of Cairo, (shahbandar al-tujjar) Isma'il Abu Taqiyya, partnered with another prominent merchant of the time and constructed two *wikalas* (commercial warehouses) on a busy and prominent location in Cairo close to the Qalawun complex, and these included a coffeehouse.[24] Nelly Hanna argues that coffee merchants encouraged the business of coffeehouses not only by sometimes constructing ones themselves but also by selling coffee to coffeehouse owners on credit, an indirect form of investment in the enterprises.[25] Merchants were not only supplying the coffee, they were also, by investing in coffeehouses, partially creating the demand.

Coffeeshops and popularization

The late Middle Ages saw the development and spread of a 'bourgeois tendency' in Arab culture.[26] This is meant to refer to a complex set of interconnected developments that overlapped and affected each other. On the one hand, literacy in its widest sense was common in the late Middle Ages. That is, a sizeable percentage, at least of the urban populations, had some ability to read and write. That in itself could have been a result of various interrelated factors: the increase in funded institutions of learning such as *kuttabs* (schools for elementary education) and *madrasas* (colleges of Islamic higher education) and hence graduates with various degrees of literacy; the spread of trade and commercialization and the need for some written communication and record keeping; and the availability of cheap paper. The cumulative result was that a wider reading public was evident; some people who were not very highly educated or who came from craft backgrounds, for example, regularly attended public reading sessions of history and religious texts and were keen to have their listening practice (*sama'at*) recorded on the manuscripts themselves.[27]

Some people who were not highly educated or at least not enough to be counted as members of the 'ulama also wrote texts during the late Middle Ages and especially the Ottoman period (fifteenth to nineteenth centuries). When they wrote, their writing was at times less polished than that of the religious scholars; they included more matters of everyday life and used more of the vernacular.[28] Some composed poetry that reflected their daily lives and included metaphors and symbols from their crafts. Some of the more learned members of society also imitated their popular colleagues: writing both sophisticated and popular texts; showing off their linguistic abilities through classical poetry but also employing popular poetic genres and metres and using the vernacular. Written culture was no longer largely confined to court circles as the middle classes came to express themselves through the genres and media previously monopolized by the cultural elite. They also expressed themselves in other, more popular genres.

Coffeeshops soon became sites for the performance of various literary arts that would not have found much space in public before. New types of public entertainment were created. It is not coincidental, perhaps, that popular epics soared in their popularity during this period and they were often performed at coffeeshops. Storytelling is of course ancient, in the Middle East as elsewhere. But the majority of specifically Arab folk epics that are known to us, such as Sirat 'Antara, Sirat al-Zahir Baybars, al-Sira al-Hilaliyya and Sirat Dhat al-Himma, as well as the Alf Layla wa Layla (*One Thousand and One Nights*) corpus, took their classical form during the late Middle Ages. Various reports confirm that reciters and performers of the *siyar* (folk epics) took coffeeshops as their main performance venues. Indeed, it is difficult to decide which came first: did the existence of coffeeshops encourage the crystallization of these narrative traditions? Or were coffeeshops needed to accommodate these new arts? Were the *siyar* performed in a different way in coffeeshops than they had been previously, perhaps at the markets, in *mulids* (saints' festivals) and public festivals or in mosques? Did the space of the coffeeshop allow for particular developments in the epics? Did the informal nature of coffeeshops allow for the rise of certain forms of expression, in poetry, music, song and dance?[29] These are some of the questions which still need further study and investigation by popular culture scholars.

The Arabic popular epics were of a fluid performative nature. The audience was usually part of the story. And while the basic parameters of the narrative were known, a performer could and did narrate individual stories within the grand cycle differently depending on the context and the reception of the audience. Narrators could and did either prolong or redact a narrative, alter the flow of events, or even add characters to satisfy a particular public.[30] The space of the coffeeshop allowed for this flexibility. Since a coffeeshop was a permanent, standing structure, a performer could divide up the narrative over several days or nights, knowing that an audience would be there each time. Unlike stories narrated within a religious setting such as a mosque or a *madrasa*, epics could include more lewd vignettes without risking the wrath of the pious in the same manner. Unlike performances tied to an annual festival, the narrator at a coffeeshop could stretch his storytelling over several days, or even a whole season. A storyteller would often be seated on the *mastaba* (or a raised seat) against the front of a coffeeshop which allowed a wider audience in addition to the clients of the coffeeshop to follow the narrative.[31] These storytelling sessions continued well into the twentieth century, although the advent of the radio and later television significantly decreased their appeal and popularity. In Cairo, for example, the nights of the fasting month of Ramadan were an opportunity for famous storytellers like Sayyid al-Dawwi to perform al-Sira al-Hilaliyya at various sites including coffeeshops until his death in 2016. In Damascus, the famous coffeeshop al-Nawfara, located right behind the Umayyad mosque, continued to host a daily telling of Sirat al-Zahir Baybars until the early twenty-first century.

All the popular epics that were recited and narrated during the late medieval and early modern period were of a historical nature. That is, they had historical characters as their main figures and purported to be dealing with historical events. The accuracy of these narratives is grey, but their value lies more in their being a window onto the mentalities of medieval Egyptian – and Arab – populations. In referring to historical figures, the reciters of the *siyar* were also making statements about authority, power, justice – the big political questions of life. The *siyar* were therefore by necessity also vehicles of political expression and critique.

Furthermore, coffeeshops were places for members of the non-elite to enjoy other performances of singing and dancing, and to play games as al-Jaziri's early observations indicate. Centuries later, with the advent of radio and television, many people would watch television dramas at the coffeeshop, especially those who could not afford to own their own devices. They would follow news bulletins in times of crises and football matches in the era of global sports as infotainment.

The night is long

Coffeeshops and the culture surrounding them are also connected to another aspect of early modern and modern social life – namely different attitudes towards the night time.[32] Night-time was becoming a busy time of the day in some corners of the Middle East including Cairo. This is reflected in the jobs of both night watchmen and market inspectors.[33] Mustafa 'Ali, visiting Cairo in 1599, praises the night watchmen for their alertness.[34] This was especially important because the people of the city were too playful at night.[35] Kafadar, in discussing Istanbul's coffeehouses by the seventeenth century and later, comments on the increasing normalcy of night-time activities and entertainment. This is indirectly reflected in the literature of the period.

Whereas classical and medieval literature does refer to events taking place at night, these often involve private gatherings indoors or escapades, raids or expeditions that are on the edge of the admissible or altogether illegal, such as in some of the *maqamat* (fictional stories) of al-Hariri or in the stories of the *One Thousand and One Nights*. By contrast, 'the settings are somewhat differently imagined after the sixteenth century, in *meddah* [praise of the Prophet Muhammad] narratives for instance, especially by the inclusion of coffeehouses as popular venues of nocturnal public festivities with the possibility of a full sense of normalcy without having to repeatedly underline privacy or criminality as obvious aspects of living the night'.[36] Some of the popular entertainment of the period, like shadow plays, were particularly

well-suited to night-time performances. This is probably reflective of the
changing urban attitudes towards the night-time in general, and changing
practices in cities of the broader Middle East that opened up both new spaces –
such as coffeeshops – and a new era for residents. This is further reflected in
modern literature where the coffeeshop as well acts as a setting for various
dramas. This is not to suggest that coffeeshops were *only* frequented at night.
Indeed, as Mustafa 'Ali himself observed in Cairo, early-rising worshippers
also frequented coffeeshops for a morning cup that would add 'life to their
life'.[37]

Coffeeshops and political activity

Scholars who have studied the rise of coffeeshops in Europe have connected
it to the development of the public sphere and public opinion. Building on
the ideas of Jürgen Habermas, they argued that the space of the coffeeshop
which allowed for discussion and intellectual debate also allowed for the rise
of a common political narrative and a shared 'public opinion' which soon
enough expressed itself politically through collective action such as during the
French Revolution and later movements of the nineteenth century. The ideas
discussed inside coffeehouses were instrumental to modernization.

   Indeed, a similar dynamic can be gleaned in the Egyptian and Middle
Eastern experience with coffeeshops. However, the debate still rages in the
field on the extent to which similar processes can be applied to Middle Eastern
history, the perils of Eurocentric historiography that measure the histories
of other parts of the world against the European experience, the degree to
which public opinion and public space is always antagonistic to absolutist
government – and other historiographical and ideological questions. While
the theoretical implications of the term 'public space' continue to be debated,
the role of the space of coffeeshops in the sociocultural transformations of the
modern Middle East, and Egypt, cannot be disputed. Neither can its political
implications. The potentially subversive energy of men getting together in a
public or semi-public space was not lost on Ottoman authorities, for example.
From the days of Khayr Bek the *muhtasib* of Mecca up to contemporary
Cairo, authorities have repeatedly banned or shut down coffeeshops in

attempts to control the activities that take place there. Many activists recount being arrested at the coffeeshop. Others recall demonstrations and riots that started out from coffeeshops, often the congregation points for like-minded citizens.

Politics of different kinds is practiced and articulated at coffeeshops, not only of the oppositional or subversive variety. In the late Ottoman period, coffeeshops associated with the janissaries and particular regiments of the Ottoman army rose to prominence. Coffee drinking came to develop its own sophisticated rituals among the military classes and to be one of the ways in which power was exercised and expressed.[38] Coffeeshops that were known to be the meeting place of officers of a particular regiment were among the features of late Ottoman cities.[39] In addition to entertainment activities, these were also sites for some Sufi practices by the regiments as well as some policing and market inspections.[40] Military officers who by the eighteenth century had non-military business interests, could also supervise these from the headquarters of their coffeeshops.[41] It is conceivable as well that other urban groups, tradesmen of certain commodities or long-distance trade, or craftsmen of a particular craft, also tended to congregate at specific coffeeshops which acted as social clubs for their groups. They were also sites for rumour and political talk of various kinds.

Traditional coffeeshops in the modern city: The nineteenth and twentieth centuries

Just as the spread of coffeeshops in the sixteenth and seventeenth centuries was associated with the rise of the new bourgeois classes, the rise of the new *afandiyya* (young professionals educated in modern schools) and politicized professionals of the nineteenth century was also associated with coffeeshops, cafés, tea rooms and bars. The rise of modern Egypt can be traced through its coffeeshops. It is not surprising in the least that when new political movements and ideas developed among the young rising professional classes of the nineteenth century, they often congregated and met at coffeeshops. Different political figures and leaders were known to patronize various coffeeshops around the capital city, Cairo. The coffeeshop was almost a natural meeting place for people with ideas. It had already established itself as such a space in the three preceding centuries. It was also already a place where people gossiped and exchanged news and rumours.

It is well-known that the printing press boomed in provinces of the Ottoman Empire in the nineteenth century, paving the way for a new type of publishing. Newspapers, magazines and different types of periodicals were printed in the different Arabic-speaking cities. Coffeeshops were among the places where the published material also took on an oral life of its own. Newspaper articles were read out loud in coffeeshops and shared with a wider audience than their primary readers. They were places where new types of writing and new ideas were shared and discussed.

Unsurprisingly, authorities of the burgeoning nation-states were quickly aware of the potential of mobilization through coffeeshops and they tried to use them to their own ends. In Istanbul, Ottoman authorities began recording spy reports at least since 1840 and many of these reported on public opinion as raised through coffeehouse discussions. In a study of such spy reports, Cengiz Kirli argues that the Ottoman state was interested in knowing popular opinions, partly as they were discussed in coffeeshop gatherings, rather than in prosecuting criminals or punishing the holders of these opinions.[42] That in itself reflects a sophisticated approach by the ruling authorities. It also exposes the inherent double danger of frequenting a coffeeshop. The presence of an informant or spy stationed at local coffeeshops would later become a recurrent scene in modern literature and films.

Narratives of important political junctures in Egyptian history, from the last quarter of the nineteenth century onwards during the twentieth, refer to various scenes having taken place in coffeeshops and to particular coffeehouses as being the congregation points of this or that political leader and his clique. At that point – as always – the cultural and the political were heavily intertwined. Over time, different types of coffeeshops developed as the city grew. Some were more modern and more Westernized, closer to cafés, others more traditional and referred to as 'baladi' or traditional. Differences related to the clientele, the location, the layout of the establishment and also to the activities that took place inside. Yet, some entertainment patterns overlapped. For example, performances of popular epics and forms of entertainment continued to take place in coffeeshops well into the early twentieth century, including at some of the 'Franji' cafés like 'Bar' al-Liwa, 'Bar' al-Anglo and the ones on Fuad I (26 July), Emad Elddin and Alfi streets, in the newly developed neighbourhoods of the modern downtown of Cairo.[43]

Recounting childhood memories in the Cairo 'Abdin quarter which developed around the newly built khedieval palace of 'Abdin since the 1860s, writer and historian Abdel Mon'eim Shemeis mentions that there were several coffeeshops known for hosting performers of the Hilaliyya epic. In the quarter of al-Qal'a (the Citadel) a poet was famous for recounting Sirat 'Antar, while another in Harat al-'Ataba off Mohammad Ali Street was famous for telling the epic of Dhat al-Himma.[44] In a neighbourhood of downtown Cairo with many Greek residents, the *hakawati* (storyteller) narrated the Hilaliyya in both Arabic and Greek![45] As a child, Shemeis would hang around the entrance to catch a few lines of the singing poets before being caught by his parents.[46] This impression of the popular, *baladi*, coffeeshop (or *ahwa*), is one that would prevail for decades afterwards and be reflected in works of literature, song and film. It is a place that was open to the street, decidedly masculine and traditional, a place to serve drinks but not food or dessert and a place that was not appropriate for families, certainly not for children, to frequent. The attitude also applied for a while to the popular forms of entertainment performed at the coffeeshop, as opposed to the newer, more modern genres such as theatre, cinema, opera or concert singing which were perceived to be part of 'high' culture and 'more respectable'.

In remembering his childhood memories, Shemeis tells about a number of popular arts that were performed at or around coffeeshops. In addition to the popular epics, there were clown shows, referred to as *Butu' ramaz*; men and women who coloured their faces in makeup and performed acrobats on the streets outside coffeeshops while narrating short stories.[47] These short stories or vignettes usually referred in a comical fashion to issues and problems of daily life.[48] Stories of the early twentieth century often referred to the injustices faced by locals at the hands of foreigners, for example. These references to the politics of everyday life were also reflected in the narrations of the *hakwatis*, the traditional storytellers. In memoirs of the 1930s, a traditional *hakawati* is described as being in dress and appearance in sync with the clientele of the coffeeshop where he performed in the neighbourhood of Sayyida 'Aishah mosque in Cairo, recounting stories and adventures of *hashish* and opium addicts.[49] These often included the fictional character of Qaraqush, based on the historical figure who was the minister of Salah al-Din al-Ayyubi (Saladin) and who is often presented in popular folktales as the paragon of unjust governance. Some of these stories are comparable to the farcical Juha stories, so popular in various countries of the Middle East.[50]

Like narratives of the folk epics and the *ramaz* and folktales, most of the arts performed at the coffeeshops were oral and included both singing and rhymed prose. These include the performances of the *udabati*, for example, who sang short poems accompanied by a drum and a small troupe that acted like a chorus.[51] This form of short and light rhymed prose allowed also for social and political criticism at times. It was a form that would be reborn by later artists like the duo Sheikh Imam and Ahmad Fu'ad Negm in the 1970s and 1980s.

Narratives of nineteenth- and early-twentieth-century Cairo in particular mention a number of historical coffeeshops, each recognized for their unique location and for their famous patrons. It is not surprising that some of the meetings of the intellectuals and activists who would come to be associated with the 'Urabi Revolt took place at coffeeshops, including, most famously, al-Bosta/Matatya.

Al Bosta/Matatya

Al Bosta (the word itself an Arabization of 'Post') was a coffeeshop next to the headquarters of the Egyptian Post Office in al-'Ataba square, one of the newly redeveloped areas of downtown Cairo where the Opera House was built in 1869 and close to al-Azbakiyya public park. It would later come to be called Matatya. Al Bosta's most prominent patron was Jamal al-Din al-Afghani (d.1897). Afghani was one of the most famous intellectuals and agent provocateur of late Ottoman politics. A reformist thinker, a new type of intellectual, Afghani also attempted to play political roles which prompted the Ottoman authorities to exile him. For a period of his career he resided in Egypt where he came to be idolized by several of its rising intellectual reformers of the time. Some of them, and Afghani himself, were to be associated with the 'Urabi Revolt of 1882.[52]

Afghani often sat at Matatya, surrounded by his followers and devotees.[53] It is quite fitting that meetings, discussions and salons of a political nature by the end of the nineteenth century would be taking place not only in private residences as was traditional, but also in a place both public and accessible, yet retaining some partial sense of privacy. Rather than the traditional learning circles of 'ulama that used to convene in *madrasas* – the famous Islamic studies universities of the Middle East – new circles were meeting in a new type of place, the *ahwa*. Many of the intellectuals and reformers of the day frequented Matatya coffeeshop: Mohammad 'Abduh, Sa'd Zaghloul, Mahmud Sami al-Barudi, Ibrahim al-Hilbawi, Ibrahim al-Muwaylihi, Adib Ishaq, Ya'qub Sannu' and the famous orator of the 'Urabi revolution, 'Abdallah al-Nadim.[54]

In many reports narrated about Afghani, his soirees at al-Bosta/Matatya lasted until the break of day, another aspect of coffeeshop culture that was to remain central to the rhythm of Cairene life.[55]

Bar al-Liwa

While al-Bosta/Matatya came to be associated with al-Afghani, Bar al-Liwa[56] was synonymous with the newspaper by the name *al-Liwa* published by the nationalist figure Mustafa Kamil (1874–1908). An image of Kamil was hung prominently at its entrance.[57] Perhaps ironically, another newspaper which would outlive *al-Liwa*, that is *al-Ahram*, had its historical headquarters across the street from Bar al-Liwa. Here, members of the elite classes and politicians as well as literati would gather until the early hours of the day. Journalists at *al-Ahram* newspaper were also regular clients.[58] Among its most famous patrons was the poet Hafiz Ibrahim (1871–1932), referred to as Sha'ir al-Nil (Poet of the Nile).[59] Hafiz Ibrahim, however, spent part of the day at another coffeeshop, one across from the historical building of the National Library of Egypt (Dar al-Kutub) on Mohammad Ali Street where he was appointed head of the literary section in 1911.[60] Indeed, Hafiz used the coffeeshop as an extension of his office; assistants would be seen bringing him paperwork to sign while he sat enjoying his coffee cup and shisha.[61]

That aspect of the coffeeshop as a place of conducting business was common among tradesmen and merchants. It was especially common in coastal cities and trade centres such as Alexandria where transactions of various natures would be conducted there especially before the establishment of the modern stock exchanges. In fact, in Alexandria in particular, it is common to refer to the *ahwa* as 'borsa' which is the word for 'stock exchange'. Several other coffeeshops were to become associated with writers, poets, politicians and activists in later decades of the twentieth century, including Café Riche, al-Horriyya and Zahrat al-Bustan cafés of downtown Cairo and the old al-Fishawi coffeeshop of Islamic Cairo. Like their precursors, they continue to be places of congregation, socialization and entertainment. They are often the first testing grounds of new ideas and debates.

Conclusion

Since their rise in the late fifteenth or early sixteenth century, coffeehouses have provided Cairenes – especially the adult men among them – with a new public space for various forms of sociability. Coffeehouses were of different sizes and degrees of sophistication; some no more than stalls in the market, while others were bigger and affording wider seating areas. They had in common being at street level and opening out onto the street, with customers often sitting outdoors. This openness and close proximity to the street while partaking in activities typically associated with homes such as drinking, socializing and enjoying various forms of entertainment, meant that coffeeshops have occupied a space in-between the public and the private and have allowed for new types of interactions between people. They have grown to be places for sharing news and gossip, idle talk, for entertainment and games, for looking for jobs and for conducting trade deals. They are places to express ideas with other adults, some of whom the patron knows and some he would not know. For many men, the coffeeshop can be an extension of the home, and a place of familiarity where both the waiters and the regulars know each other and develop bonds and alliances – a refuge in an occasionally harsh city.

3

Locating the *ahwa* (café) in the work of Egyptian writers

Introduction: Literature, writers and the coffeehouse

In this chapter, we move from the historical context of the emergence of the coffee drink and the coffeehouse as a space taking shape in-between the public and the private to the literary field to explore the strong bond which Egyptian writers have developed with the coffeehouse. It almost seems natural that the café space would attract the class of urban literati as they are the ones who are constantly involved in producing new ideas and concepts through their creative writing. In a BBC Radio 3 programme entitled 'Stirring up a revolution', the presenter Tarek Osman meets with the renowned Egyptian novelist Ibrahim Abdel Meguid at Café Riche[1] in June 2013, where Abdel Meguid shares his experience of the coffeehouse as follows:

> For me when I come to a café like Riche I feel that I change ... I forget everything and be calm ... I became an optimist when I started coming here. ... I came to Riche originally because Naguib Mahfouz had a meeting here every Friday. But I also met other very important and famous writers and poets like Naguib Surour, for example, Amal Dunqul, Yehia al-Taher Abdullah, Soliman Fayyad. Cafés have been places for creativity and innovation in literature as well as in politics for young generations over the past 30 or 40 years. Cafés are also places for rest and relief for writers. Sometimes they sit here at the café the whole day even for 12 hours. You cannot find freedom but at the café. ... Writers are very free in the café and speak about everything. They can protest and voice their views as they want to. ... We know that security forces send people to spy on what we say in cafés, but we don't care.[2]

Here, Abdel Meguid's sentiments about Café Riche strongly resonate with so many Egyptian and Arab writers. Broadly speaking, the relationship between the Arab coffeehouse and the production of literature and cultural activities is a historical phenomenon. Egypt, among other Arab countries like Syria, Iraq, Lebanon, Morocco and Jordan, has witnessed this strong bond between writers and their *favourite* coffeehouses, which are in many cases reflected in their literary and artistic outputs.

Throughout his study *The Production of Space*, Henri Lefebvre underlines 'space' as a social relationship and draws attention over and again to its diversity (heterogeneity). He goes on to explain that the concept of social space (particularly urban space) develops and becomes broader over time precisely because '*social spaces interpenetrate one another and/or superimpose themselves upon one another*'.[3] He further makes the following key observation, which captures, as we argue, the production of knowledge and literature through the spatial medium of the coffeehouse:

> Though a *product* to be used, to be consumed, it is also a *means of production*; networks of exchange and flows of raw materials and energy fashion space and are determined by it. Thus this means of production, produced as such, cannot be separated either from the productive forces, including technology and knowledge, or from the social division of labour which shapes it, or from the state and the superstructures of society.[4]

In the coffeehouse, knowledge production (particularly literature) enriches the writer's experience of storytelling and provides him/her with the narrative space for the development of characters. This knowledge is then transmitted beyond the space of the café to reach the outside world. In this sense, literature has the power to create layers of spaces through the intertwining of the characters' lives, thus underscoring what Lefebvre has referred to as the 'unlimited multiplicity or unaccountable set of social spaces'.[5] This is significant because it helps us understand the complexity of particular urban spaces such as the coffeehouse that shape the writer's imagination and add a unique angle of interpretation to Lefebvre's theory on the production of space and relations. In the following analysis, we will demonstrate the extent to which the social space of the coffeehouse has influenced the fictional works of Egyptian writers.

In the introductory chapter, we have emphasized the fact that academic research lags behind where the analysis of café culture is concerned in Egyptian society despite the centrality of this place in urban living. However, one of the crucial findings we have depicted through our research points to the enormous permeation of the image and representation of the traditional café and the historical-cultural coffeehouse in the literary works of Egyptian writers, particularly novels, short stories, testimonies and memoirs. The *ahwa baladi* specifically is so present in a large volume of literature of the modern period to the point of being a constant feature of city life. Its aura is woven into the fabric of the city, most notably Cairo, inhabited by characters from all walks of life. Therefore, it would be an impossible task for the researcher to include *all* the literary works which have portrayed the café in one form or another.

In an archive of articles (compiled in 2011), the online Arabic Matar Literary Forum has documented the relationship between novelists, poets, journalists and artists from across the Arab world (as producers) and the café (as a social and cultural space) while providing the reader with much information about the history of many coffeehouses in Cairo, Baghdad, Damascus, Beirut, Amman, Jeddah and other cities through a literary lens.[6] In this online archive, the late Egyptian novelist Gamal al-Ghitani wrote a story entitled 'Katib wa makan' (A writer and a place), where he reflects on al-Fishawi coffeehouse,[7] a historic and cultural place in al-Hussein area in Old Cairo.[8] He reminisces about how this coffeehouse was the only one known in Cairo, long time ago, to open its doors for twenty-four hours a day. Al Ghitani says that the place was always filled with writers, artists, journalists and actors who would frequent it late at night after finishing their work and would assemble there until the early morning hours. The night is always long for the literati. Since al-Ghitani himself was a resident of al-Gamaliyya neighbourhood, not far from Fishawi, he used to visit it at any time of the day. In his tale, he provides vivid descriptions of its atmospheric ambience and its old owner Haj Fahmi al-Fishawi who died in 1969 just before his coffeehouse was knocked down following an absurd decision issued by the Cairo governor at the time. Al Ghitani remembers how a huge campaign was launched by writers and artists to revoke this decision, but to al-Ghitani's great dismay they could not stop the old Fishawi coffeehouse from being demolished. Later on, a new smaller Fishawi would be built in the same corner in al-Hussein, which still exists until the present day. Al Ghitani decided to immortalize the image and richness of the old coffeehouse in a short story he published in 1991 entitled 'The Coffeehouse and Its Owner'.[9]

Al Ghitani writes about how coffeehouses share similar functions: they are places where male friends meet to enjoy the freedom of laughing, chatting and joking aloud so as to evade the restrictions placed within their households where they have to be quiet in the presence of their parents, spouses or children. He goes on to say that many men also meet at the coffeehouse to do business or to find small jobs, such as in the case of construction workers who rely on a daily wage or government employees who pass by the *ahwa* in the morning to have a drink before going to work. For him as a novelist, he remarks, he always found these functions of the coffeehouse rather fascinating:

> The coffeehouses take people to different spaces, and people depart from them. The coffeehouses are the ports of the city and the corners of its secrets. The Cairene considers the coffeehouse as a centre of identity, so he says: 'I am going to *my* café.' He speaks proudly of his group of friends at the coffeehouse, as it is a support network as well as a refuge for him.[10]

Interestingly, the reader will find echoes of al-Ghitani's quote in the testimonies by our interviewees in Chapter 7 which indicates the extent to which the coffeehouse is perceived as a marker of social identity for many Egyptians. In his story, al-Ghitani gives examples of a number of coffeehouses around Cairo, the ones which mostly caught his attention. He captures the ways in which the writer in particular is attracted to *his* favourite coffeehouse. Indeed, the coffeehouse has been represented in modern Egyptian literature by *male* authors, most notably the Nobel laureate Naguib Mahfouz, but also by other famous novelists such as Khairy Shalabi, Mohammad al-Bisati, Ibrahim Aslan, Youssef Idris, Sonallah Ibrahim and Ibrahim Abdel Meguid, precisely in order to detect the significance of the coffeehouse in the lives of their characters. Rarely have women novelists imagined the coffeehouse in their fiction, hence the novelistic genre is yet to see this development in future works.

In another writer's experience, the veteran Egyptian novelist Sonallah Ibrahim captures the important role of Café Riche, originally of Greek ownership, and located in the heart of downtown Cairo on Talaat Harb Street, saying that 'it was the meeting place for intellectuals during and after the [nineteen] sixties.'[11] What further ascertained its influence on the trajectory of many writers and journalists, both men and women, was the fact that novelist Naguib Mahfouz used to go there every morning to drink coffee and read the papers (as mentioned in the introductory chapter). Ibrahim reminisces about Café Riche in the 1960s and 1970s because he considers this period to be its 'golden age',

> when it used to bustle with the most vital literary debates: committed literature, social realism, and the absurd, when small literary journals, some of which never saw the light (or did for a short while) would be concocted at its tables, when film scripts and plays would be discussed in small groups, and when many were taken to detention camps or prisons because of a word or a joke recorded in a secret report, written at a neighbouring table.[12]

Later on, Café Riche would close down in the aftermath of the 1992 earthquake and then reopen in 1999 after refurbishment work. The place still stands today in its original location in downtown Cairo, with its transformed ambience from the description provided by Ibrahim in the above quote. However, its owners have kept the old room where famous writers and poets used to meet as separate from the main restaurant, and where we see pictures of iconic literary figures, artists and singers hung on its walls as a testament to its rich cultural history.

After closing down the café, as Sonallah Ibrahim goes on to say, these writers had to 'relocate' to other cafés in downtown, one of which was Zahrat al-Bustan, located on a back street at a close proximity to Riche.[13] Al Bustan used to be a meeting point for the less-privileged classes such as doormen, drivers and street vendors. Thus, this small café witnessed a new momentum after the 'intellectual' class started frequenting it. Ibrahim gives this issue of relocation a humorous twist when he says that the writers kept expanding their presence around the downtown cafés until they formed what he refers to as the 'Triangle of Horror'. This begins at Zahrat al-Bustan café, then extending north of Café Riche on one side to Le Grillon restaurant and coffeeshop;[14] and extending to the east of Riche to reach the Odeon bar and coffeeshop on the roof of Odeon Hotel. This triangle has constituted landmarks for writers, journalists and artists as well as political activists and opposition figures for so many years.[15] The description 'Triangle of Horror' alludes to the heated political and cultural debates which were widespread in these places in the 1980s and 1990s, and which put many figures at risk of being arrested and jailed. Yet, the role which these coffeehouses have played as cultural places and social entertainment venues still stands to the present day.

In an interview with writer and poet Ibrahim Daoud, he said that he perceives Zahrat al-Bustan café as the 'conscience of cultural life in Cairo' because it has been open for writers and poets from all over Egypt.[16] Those young and unknown literati figures who came from different provinces whether in the north or south of Egypt to Cairo the megacity, met with prominent writers first at Zahrat al-Bustan café because of its cheap prices and its openness, before moving to other cafés. Daoud himself still frequents Zahrat al-Bustan and reminisces about how he and other poets, most notably the late Amal Dunqul, used to compose and recite their poetry at this café and others in the downtown area, while reaching out to their friends and readers through literary and political debates.[17] Zahrat al-Bustan has a proud phrase displayed at the top of its doors: 'A meeting place for artists and writers'.

In his collection entitled *al-Gaww al-'Amm* (The General Ambience),[18] Daoud writes short stories about many friends and acquaintances he has known in Cairo, the city he moved to decades ago from his hometown in the Delta. He is a public figure, poet, writer and journalist at *al-Ahram* newspaper and he spends much of his social time at the Cairo downtown cafés. In this collection of short stories, the café has a fundamental presence in the life of many people he has encountered or befriended. It appears as a 'natural' element of the urban structure, always there in the background, always taken for granted as a place that is open and accessible to the male characters at any time of the day or night. Sometimes, it is a refuge for those lonely souls in the big city who have nowhere else to go or have no family or friends, similar to the working-class character Abu Emad in story number 12 who was forced into early retirement from the prominent Iron and Steel Company in Helwan and completely lost his bearings as a result. Abu Emad appeared to be on the verge of losing his mind, talking to himself frequently, until he found a small *ahwa* on Mu'izz Street in Islamic Cairo. He started spending his time there, chatting with its owner and other customers as his only means to escape the grave disappointment and boredom in his life.

Daoud's stories are replete with cafés scattered all over Greater Cairo, the Cooks' Café, Zahrat al-Bustan, the Windsor coffeeshop and restaurant, Gomhuriyya Café, Faysal Street cafés in Giza, Café Riche and many others. It is the central stop where the characters frequently meet to have drinks, watch football matches, play games and smoke *hash* and shisha. Through these stories, one can visualize the café culture as integral to urban living due to its open, inclusive space.

In a short documentary about Zahrat al-Bustan café made by Al Jazeera Documentary Channel in 2015, the late novelist Mikkawi Sa'id reminisces about his memories of the café when he started frequenting it in the late 1970s to engage with other writers and poets, and to read and discuss each other's works.[19] Sa'id highlights how some of the new writers who arrived in Cairo from other provinces would feel at home at this particular café to the point that they received their post there. The café's address became their own. Sa'id further explains that the liberal, open ambience of the café encouraged women to frequent it as well, which was not the case with some of the other downtown cafés at the time. The close proximity of Zahrat al-Bustan to the Cairo Atelier, a landmark of intellectual life in the downtown area where cultural events and exhibitions took place on the Tuesday of every week, also led many people to gather at the café after finishing the Atelier events.

Furthermore, the renowned novelist Salwa Bakr, who belongs to the same generation as Mikkawi Sa'id, says in the film that she also started frequenting Zahrat al-Bustan in the late 1970s when she was a university student, and this particular café has played a major role in the life of her generation of writers. Young and talented writers and poets came to the café to meet with the high-profile writers of the time and discuss with them their works and listen to their public talks. She mentions that Naguib Mahfouz used to deliver a talk every Friday after the noon prayers at the café, an event which was attended by many new writers. Bakr points to how both Riche and Zahrat al-Bustan were also famous among other writers from different parts of the Arab world who came to meet with their Egyptian colleagues, especially during such important annual events as the Cairo Book Fair. The veteran film-maker Magdi Ahmed Ali, also interviewed in this short documentary, adds another reason for the popularity of Zahrat al-Bustan. He mentions that the place transcends social and class barriers in the way that it is open to everyone and even the prestigious writers and artists who frequent it sit side by side with ordinary people. Ali underlines this point as a distinct characteristic of the café.

Significance of coffee and coffeehouse in a selection of literary works

In this part, we focus on a selection of representations of the café in literary works and analyse their broader cultural implications. In his novella *Al Maqha al-Zujaji* (The Glass Coffeehouse, 1979),[20] novelist and short story writer Mohammad al-Bisati provides a narrative about Turkish characters who live in a small, unnamed Egyptian village where the coffeehouse is their main meeting point. It is suggested that the time of the tale is the later part of the nineteenth century when many Turks preferred to stay in Egypt rather than go back to Turkey after the advent of the British colonial regime in 1882. Al Bisati is known for writing mostly about village life in rural Egypt, and in this novella he portrays his protagonists as old male characters, who are about to die, thus suggesting metaphorically that the authority of the Ottoman Empire itself was fading away. The old age of his characters alludes to the 'sick man of Europe', a description which referred to the Ottoman Empire in its later days.

The coffeehouse in this novella is characterized by its huge glass windows which overlook the main railway station in this anonymous village, and it is owned by an old Turkish migrant. It is the main point where Turks who live in the village and the neighbouring towns gather in the evenings to drink brandy and cognac, play cards and exchange news about their friends and relatives who live far away or in Turkey. It is interesting here that these *khawagat* (foreigners), as being referred to by the locals, are depicted by the colonized subject, that is the Egyptian novelist, who looks back at this era in Egypt's history and reconstructs portraits of the colonizer. The narrative shows how some of the Turks 'hid' in those remote Egyptian villages to escape from punishment for crimes they might have committed in their own country. In

Egypt, they managed to accumulate wealth and build large beautiful houses surrounded by gardens. Al Bisati depicts these images in the text and situates the wealthy Turks as opposed to the Egyptian villagers who are suffering from hunger and poverty. We see here how the coffeehouse serves as a safe haven for the Turks where they form a bond of fraternity.

Al Bisati's novella raises questions about the way in which the coffeehouse can be fictionalized to address political issues. The Turkish coffeehouse and what take place there are the driving force of the narrative. While commenting on the role of the coffeehouse in modern Arabic literature, the literary critic Mustapha al-Dab' observes that fiction writers started to create representations of the coffeehouse when it became a 'reality' and had a strong presence in the lives of the cities and towns they inhabited. Hence, their representations aimed to accentuate the social and political role of the coffeehouse in the lives of their characters.[21] In his view, by portraying the coffeehouse as integral to the narrative structure, the Arab writer has also established an 'aesthetic' function of the place.[22]

In another highly acclaimed novella *Siraj* (translated into English as *Siraaj: An Arab Tale*),[23] the late novelist and scholar Radwa Ashour situates her tale in a fictional island off the coast of Yemen in the late nineteenth century. The story revolves around Amina and her young son Sa'id who leaves the island in his early teens in search of work where he finds himself at the shores of Alexandria during the 1881–2 'Urabi Revolt. Sa'id witnesses the bombing of Alexandria by the British troops who arrived in the city in July 1882 to crush the revolt, hence initiating their colonial rule of Egypt for the next seventy years. Sa'id spends several years in Egypt but later returns to his island as a grown-up man. After his return, he becomes involved in an underground movement together with the slaves and poor-stricken fishermen on the island against their despotic sultan – while adopting for their movement the secret word 'siraj' (the Arabic word for 'lamp' or 'light').

Upon Sa'id's return to the island, he brings back with him an unknown 'substance', coffee beans, which he was introduced to in Egypt during his travels. At the start, his mother Amina refuses to taste this substance claiming that it is intoxicating and has been forbidden by the religious authority of the island. As the omniscient narrator tells:

Sa'id brought it upon his return from his travels and when she [Amina] opened the bag and saw the green beans, she did not know what it was so she asked him. He replied:

– Coffee

– Coffee?

– Yes.

– But it is *haram* (forbidden).

– Who said so?

– The judge issued a *fatwa* (religious statement) and said that it is a *bid'a* (heresy) and any heresy is misguided and any misguidance leads to hell. And the caller announced on the island that coffee is forbidden by the sultan's order and that its name is derived from alcohol and it makes the person drunk and is intoxicating, and blurs the brains and whoever drinks it will be punished by 100 lashes.[24]

This news bewilders Sa'id so he tries to reassure his mother that coffee is not *haram* and that people drink it in Egypt, and grow it and trade in it in Yemen, and that no one else has forbidden it except the tyrannical sultan of their island. However, the news travels fast and people start gossiping about Sa'id who has come back carrying the forbidden coffee. But gradually, Amina has become convinced by her son's story and starts drinking coffee with him fearlessly. Sa'id thinks to himself that the slaves on the island have started growing the coffee beans behind the sultan's back, and now everyone is drinking and enjoying it. Drinking coffee comes to be a rebellious act carried out by the underprivileged class who are plotting to overthrow the sultan and his regime. By highlighting how coffee emerges as the favourite drink among the rebels, the novelist also establishes it as a 'symbol' of resistance against the dictator's authority and control: 'The sultan does not know that his slaves drink coffee and are plotting to dethrone him.'[25]

Siraj creates a link between the Egyptians' revolt against foreign intervention in 1882 and the slaves' revolt on this unnamed island, where the British have also allied with the sultan and founded a military base by the sea. The revolt is defeated when the British open fire from the sea at the demonstrators and Sa'id dies fighting in it, similar to the defeat of 'Urabi's army in the battle of al-Tall al-Kabir by the British forces in September 1882. This fictional link underscores a lineage between the oppressed classes in any place within any period of time, who rise to fight for social justice and freedom against their oppressors. The novella can be perceived as an allegory that embraces the universal aspiration of emancipation from humiliation and injustice. The twist here is that the novelist imagines the coffee drink as something inspiring which is adopted specifically by the rebels during their fight against the oppressors' class.

And thus, this was the beginning of the coffee drink for many people, an act of subversion, as alluded to in Chapter 2 of this book. Perhaps one of the most satiric Egyptian writers who presented the traditional café in a humorous manner is Mahmoud al-Sa'dani. In several of his collections of comical and witty tales, al-Sa'dani locates many of them in one specific place in Giza: *qahwet* al-Mo'allim Katkut (the café of Master Katkut). Within this lively, dynamic setting, the writer reveals through real-life situations, encounters and conversations, the ways in which the café played such a decisive and formative role in his writing career while providing him with numerous themes and portraits of people from the marginalized, bottom layer of Egyptian society. In his 'introduction' to al-Sa'dani's collection *Hikayat Qahwet Katkut* (The Tales of Katkut Café),²⁶ the well-known Egyptian novelist Mohammad Mustagab writes about al-Sa'dani's skill in delving into the popular and street culture of Cairo and Giza to bring to the reader's imagination larger-than-life characters whom he met at the café. Mustagab refers to al-Sa'dani's pen as 'writing at the ground level' to underscore his vast knowledge of and fraternity with working-class communities in urban Egypt, and his portrayal of their daily heroism in making a living while using their own style of vernacular expressions and jokes. In other words, al-Sa'dani could not find in the classical Arabic language the relevant lexical register to capture how the working classes go about their daily business and how they converse with one another. He found his medium of expression through the vernacular, and where else to situate his characters but within their most familiar setting, the traditional café. These choices made his writing far more realistic, accessible and relatable to his target readership: the popular classes.

In the first lines of *The Tales of Katkut Café*, al-Sa'dani paints this telling picture of his favourite café:

> Even though Katkut Café had the same image of other cafés spread across Egypt, it was indeed a microcosm of the whole of Egypt. In contrast to all other cafés, it changed its skin several times a day. In the early morning,

lawyers' assistants frequented it, together with groups of peasants who came to the city to attend their court tribunals. And in the afternoon, those students who skipped their classes came to sit at the café, in addition to the workers at the Mizrahi cinema studio [Mizrahi was a Jewish Italian filmmaker who lived and worked in Egypt]. Sometimes, groups of boys and young men would gather in front of the café to watch the amateur actors who sat there waiting to play their roles in front of the camera. The underprivileged sectors of Giza looked at these actors as if they were stars. … And at sunset, government employees, high-profile and less so, would gather at the café.[27]

After the government employees leave the café at around eleven in the evening, other types of customers arrive, writers and journalists, whose voices are louder and presence more pronounced. Moreover, university students also frequented the café in the evening and met with their professors to discuss political issues. These groups would spend hours at the café until sunrise. And during all these hours, the café owner, Master Katkut, sits around overseeing the business and smoking his shisha. And such was the daily sequence at Katkut café, ongoing, energetic and full of life and noise. Al Sa'dani goes on to describe in detail these different groups of men and how they all come to tell their tales and entertain themselves at the café where barriers between classes drop, and where they find themselves connecting and conversing at ease and comfort. This was a time in the city just before the breakout of WWII, as al-Sa'dani's objective here is to show how the war impacted the lives of the café's characters while extending the metaphor of the café to the whole of Egypt.

The café as a 'character' in Ahmed Mourad's *1919* and Ibrahim Aslan's *The Heron*

Another novel which highlights the political role of the traditional *ahwa* as well as the historical-cultural coffeehouse during a crucial period of Egypt's modern revolutionary history is Ahmed Mourad's *1919*, which was published in the aftermath of the January 2011 revolution.[28] The novel reconstructs the events during and after the 1919 popular revolution when the masses across Egypt went on the streets against the British colonial regime demanding independence and the return to Egypt of their much revered leader Sa'd Zaghloul from his forced exile in Malta. Mourad brings into the narrative real historical figures such as Zaghloul himself; his wife Safiyya Zaghloul who was respected and loved by the people; the sultan Ahmed Fouad who ruled Egypt after Khedive Abbas Helmi and had his son Farouq ascend to the throne after him; Queen Nazli, the sultan's wife and Farouq's mother; Badi'a Masabni, the iconic dancer and singer who owned the nightclub Café Égyptiennes; in addition to real freedom fighters who were involved in the underground armed movement against the British and the sultan, such as Ahmed Abdel Hayy Kira. Mourad populates the narrative with a diverse range of characters, some real and others fictional to map out this specific historic era in Egypt and the political transformations which were taking place then and which shaped the following decades until the Free Officers carried out their coup in 1952 and ended both the monarchy and the colonial period.

Within this intricate plot of historical detail, the novelist focuses on the armed underground group that was called 'The Black Hand', and whom Ahmed Kira belonged to. Kira had lost his father when he was executed by the British colonialists because he was one of Ahmed 'Urabi's followers during the 1882 Revolt. Through linking the 'Urabi Revolt and the 1919 revolution, the novelist creates a historical and political lineage and highlights two decisive events in the Egyptians' struggle against occupation and foreign intervention. Ahmed Kira believes that he is continuing what 'Urabi and his supporters (including his own father) had started when they set off to fight the British occupiers in 1882. Mourad recreates the place which has brought these two generations together around the issue of national independence: Matatya Café located in the popular area of al-'Ataba in downtown Cairo, close to the old Opera House.

As discussed in Chapter 2, Matatya Café (or al-Bosta) is known for being the place where the scholar and philosopher Jamal al-Din al-Afghani met with his friends and students to debate issues about nationalism and independence during the latter part of the nineteenth century on the eve of 'Urabi's Revolt. Al Afghani is known to have invigorated the national sentiments of his followers with his strong, eloquent speeches leading them to embrace the revolution against the Ottomans and foreign occupiers. Such historical figures as the religious scholar Mohammad 'Abduh, writer and journalist 'Abdallah al-Nadim and poet Mahmud Sami al-Barudi also met with Afghani at Matatya: 'From this small café, the wind of future revolutions has set off, and on its old chairs the protagonists of these revolutions sat, not quite knowing yet which direction to take.'[29] The iconic café was demolished in the late twentieth century, but the stories and memories of its pioneers have been immortalized in history books and literary works.[30]

In Mourad's novel, the writer establishes how Sa'd Zaghloul himself frequented Matatya as a young man together with 'Urabi's supporters to plot against the foreign occupiers and mobilize for the revolt. In the year 1919, we see Ahmed Kira, symbolizing a new generation of freedom fighters, meeting at the same café with his fellow comrades in the underground movement to plan for their operations on the eve of the revolution and in its aftermath. He keeps with him an old photograph of his father and Sa'd Zaghloul standing together and smiling in one corner of the café. In this sense, Matatya is reconceived in the novel as a political space where revolutionary fervour was produced and transferred from one generation to the next. The reader can even visualize its revolutionary role, personified as a character, juxtaposed to others in the novel.

Mourad also revives in the reader's imagination Café Riche as the place where members of The Black Hand organization met in the basement (or the wine cellar) and carried out their operations, writing and printing political statements and thousands of leaflets. During the 1919 revolution and its aftermath, Café Riche stands as an icon of the people's place that supported the revolutionaries and hosted their activism for independence. The novelist introduces us to the Greek owner of Riche at the time, Michael Nicolapolits who opened the place as a restaurant and bar, and had an extension which stretched outdoors onto the garden and hosted a theatre where the most famous singers and actors performed, including Umm Kulthoum, Mounira al-Mahdiyya and Mohammad Abdel Wahab. The owner believed in the Egyptian national struggle against the British and sultan Fouad and facilitated the revolutionaries' work by allowing them to hide in the basement. We are introduced to this legendary café in the following lines:

> Downtown .. Café Riche. The name is written in a beautiful calligraphy at the top of the front glass door, opposite the garden that stretches to Soliman Pasha Square [later to be called Talaat Harb Square]. The tables have been arranged on the green grass and covered by white cloth and shiny glasses on

the top. The customers are sitting around them listening to the music of a small band playing a piece by Mozart.

Since the start of the war [WWI], this café which overlooks Soliman Pasha Square has become the meeting place of the middle classes who belong to the opposition from all different ideologies, men of letters, poets, theatre actors and journalists, and where seminars are held and plays and musicals are performed on its small theatre stage. At the same time, it is also the gathering place of spies and informers! Those who are hunting for the nationalists that express their views in public.[31]

It is at Café Riche that Ahmed Kira, a prominent member of The Black Hand organization, explains to Abdel Qader Shehata, the ordinary semi-educated citizen, what is expected of him as an activist in the national struggle. In the basement where the revolutionaries issue and print their political leaflets, Abdel Qader will fall in love, for the first time in his life, with Dawlat, the young school teacher who left her village in Minya to come to Cairo on her own and join the struggle. It is in this underground room, with its stifled air and tense atmosphere filled with news of those who have been killed and wounded by the British on the demonstrations, that Abdel Qader will feel at peace and harmony with himself after a life journey of loss, violence and alienation. In the basement of Riche, we get to know the members of this small cell, who come across as a microcosm of the nation itself, their uncompromising political commitment and their ultimate sacrifices for the national cause of independence. The novelist saturates the story with 'thriller' events, the narrative genre that Mourad excels in as we have read in his previous novels, particularly *Vertigo* (2007) and *The Blue Elephant* (2012). In this way, Mourad situates Riche at the heart of the plot, a symbolic 'character' that embraces others, while revealing its extraordinary influence in the lives of the revolutionaries. As the narrative establishes a political lineage between 'Urabi's Revolt and the 1919 revolution symbolized by the two iconic meeting places of the revolutionaries in Matatya and Café Riche, it also alludes to the continuity of the popular struggle movement which reached yet a new high point with the breakout of the January 2011 revolution.

However, despite Mourad's welcome attempt to shed light on and unpack many forgotten stories by recreating real figures associated with the 1919 revolutionary wave, he fails to present to the reader in-depth characterization and rather delves into a descriptive and melodramatic mode that undermines the complexity of the historical events themselves. In some dialogues between the characters, one cannot escape imagining them as caricatures in an Egyptian soap opera. Literary critic Dina Heshmat points out that the novel lacks a 'revolutionary soul' despite the 'brave re-historicization' that the author experiments with in uncovering many significant events during and after the 1919 momentum.[32] Heshmat goes on to say that perhaps one of the main achievements of the novel lies in the links it creates between several revolutionary moments in Egypt's modern history, beginning with the 'Urabi Revolt and arriving at 1919 and then the events of 1922 when the Egyptians rose again against the British but this time they also used the most effective weapon of boycotting all British goods and produce.[33]

Whereas *1919* chronicles a crucial revolutionary period in the early part of twentieth-century Egypt and reimagines the key political role which specific cafés played in the life of revolutionaries, in his widely acclaimed novel *Malik al-Hazin* (*The Heron*), published in 1983,[34] novelist Ibrahim Aslan situates his main male characters living in the working-class Cairene area of Imbaba within the social space of the neighbourhood's café. The events take place on the eve of another defining political movement in 1970s' Egypt: the mass bread riots of 18 and 19 January 1977 against President Anwar Sadat's decision to lift the government subsidy on basic food items. Aslan himself lived in Imbaba and wrote most of his stories about this place,[35] thus attaching a 'historical memory' to it. In *The Heron*, Aslan personifies Awadallah Café, the main *ahwa baladi* in the neighbourhood, while describing it as a 'living being' that feels joy and pain similar to its customers. Aslan aims to make Awadallah Café vivid in our imagination, precisely because its demise serves as an allegory for the loss of many things of value in Egypt in the late 1970s: homes, morals, jobs and friendships. Mirroring the people who found themselves 'betrayed' and left behind by the state, Aslan's narrative revolves around the imminent day when Awadallah Café would be passed on to its new owner, *Mo'allim* (master) Sobhi, a *nouveau riche* businessman who made his wealth by selling chickens and dealing drugs. Like many others who accumulated fast wealth as a result of President Anwar Sadat's economic open-door policy in the early 1970s, Mo'allim Sobhi wants to demolish the whole building where the café occupies the ground floor in order to build a big block of flats. He is seen by one of the characters as a 'cancer which is spreading everywhere in their alley, buying old houses and demolishing them'.[36]

Aslan portrays Awadallah Café as analogous to others that we come across in working-class neighbourhoods in Cairo, where groups of men gather around the wooden tables to listen to the radio, play domino, enjoy hot and cold drinks, smoke hash and shisha and exchange news about the country. Once again, the café is the central point of this backstreet where all the important conversations between characters take place and where the key actions are set. Abdullah, the café's *qahwagi* (waiter), moves swiftly around the tables as usual to serve the customers. It is often made clear in narratives about coffeehouses that the ones who know the secrets of the place are the waiters, because they listen all the time to the customers' gossip and chats. This is also the case here through the portrayal of Abdullah's character.

Yet, Abdullah is not any waiter, but one who has come to age with the café itself. He was employed by the previous owner long time ago since the café was first opened. Thus, he feels it is his home: 'This place became a café and I became a waiter at the same time, together. ... If there is no Awadallah Café, there is no Abdullah.'[37] He thinks to himself: 'So what am I going to do? When I get up in the morning and I don't come here, where shall I go? And how am I going to make a living?'[38] In this way, Aslan complicates the relationship between the café and Abdullah the waiter who is attached to it as his own home. This relationship reinforces its image as symbolic of the country (part of a whole) that is bearing witness to its own demise on the hands of a new class of businessmen whose wealth is accumulated through drug smuggling.

It is through this ongoing conflict over the café, a narrative strategy which Aslan employs as a metaphor for the economic and political transformations that Egypt was going through in the 1970s, that the reader is able to unpack the 'aesthetic' function of the café in the novel. The author makes the café the focal point where the characters' stories are told and where new relationships are forged; it is portrayed as the place which embraces these tales. As critic Mustapha al-Dab' remarks: 'Aslan created the café to be the memory which preserves the nation's history. ... He associates the loss of the café with the loss of the people and their history.'[39] Gradually, as the stories grow in complexity and entanglements, the reader comes to realize that a 'grand narrative' about the Imbaba people and their everyday struggles is being told and celebrated: the deep bonds of friendships and fraternity between the neighbours; the humour and sarcasm which characterize their conversations; the optimism about life and love despite the economic hardships and poor standards of living; and the larger-than-life characters such as the blind Sheikh Hosni, ʿAmm ʿOmran (who knows by heart the whole history of Imbaba because he has lived through it), and Abdullah the waiter. In Aslan's novel, we see how the café shelters the characters and their stories, and how they in turn do their best to keep it alive.

But to the characters' enormous dismay (as well as the reader's), the café closes down and Moʿallim Sobhi turns it into a place where he slaughters the chickens and sells them. This image of cutting the chickens into pieces to be sold is intensified and described in detail in the novel – 'the café has been stabbed'[40] – thus suggesting that it was not only the café that was disfigured in such a violent way, but in fact the whole country as well, as the riots against the government also intensify in the later part of the novel. Millions of people across Egypt went on riots on 18 and 19 January 1977 against Sadat's decision of lifting the subsidies; and in retaliation, the Central Security Forces were deployed to shoot live bullets at the demonstrators and fire teargas to disperse them. We read in the novel how some of the characters get caught in the clashes when the forces reach *midan* al-Kitkat (the main square in Imbaba). We see how Youssef al-Naggar, one of the main protagonists, spends the first night of the riots collecting the empty teargas canisters before he reads their labels to realize they were made in the United States. The novel ends with Youssef deciding to join the demonstrators. A new political dynamic in the country was set off and it was not possible to contain it.

In *The Heron*, the characters who frequent Awadallah Café are indeed a sector of the 'subaltern' population, whose way of life captures the notion of creating an 'art of presence' (highlighted in the introductory chapter), which scholar Asef Bayat elaborates in his article 'Politics in the city-inside-out'.[41] Here, Bayat refers to 'the subaltern capacity to recognize their limitations, and yet understand and discover opportunities and inventive methods of practice, in order to take advantage of the available spaces to resist and move on'.[42] Through their 'everyday lifeworlds', Aslan's characters shed light on urban living when the country was turning into a neoliberal economy, and how it feels to experience such economic and political transformation during the Sadat era. They are the bottom layer of the city, the unemployed, the marginalized and those who live on casual and informal work – thus the consequences of the economic hardships including inflation and loss of homes and jobs had their worst impact on them.

Conclusion

Through shedding light on a selection of literary works by well-known Egyptian writers, the aim of this chapter has been to investigate the diversity in representing the coffeehouse in literature as well as to explore the formidable and long-lasting relation of Egyptian writers to their favourite cafés. As café culture became a reality in the writers' lives who inhabit cities, the *ahwa baladi* in particular has had a constant presence in an enormous output of modern Egyptian literature. This in itself serves as a key signifier for its centrality in the production and development of urban space. Literature best captures the coffeehouse as a 'social space' and transcends it to move freely into a multiplicity of other social spaces while dissecting cultural, political and historical relations. Yet, despite these rich and multifaceted representations by many novelists and short story writers (mostly male figures), it was indeed Naguib Mahfouz, more than anyone else, who had brought to our collective popular imagination the cultural, spatial and political significance of the coffeehouse through his novels as well as his own lifestyle. It would not be an exaggeration to state that both the *ahwa baladi* and the modern, cultural coffeehouse figure in most of Mahfouz's works. As al-Dabʿ suggests, Mahfouz created what can be referred to as 'the novel of the coffeehouse'.[43] In fact, the Mahfouzian coffeehouse comes to resemble an autonomous social and economic unit in itself that defines urban living in various ways, as will be demonstrated in the next chapter.

4

The case of Naguib Mahfouz: Storyteller of the Egyptian coffeehouse

Introduction: The coffeehouse theme in Naguib Mahfouz's fiction

In this chapter, and as a way to build on our arguments in the previous chapter, we analyse representations of the coffeehouse in a selection of Mahfouz's works to study the ways in which widely read literary texts have fictionalized the coffeehouse as an integral part of Egyptian urban space. The works and representations in this chapter serve as *samples* to signify broader issues during key periods of Egypt's modern history in the twentieth century. We argue that Mahfouz is perceived here as *the* 'storyteller' or 'literary chronicler' par excellence of the Egyptian coffeehouse. For him, the coffeehouse resembles a 'character', one whose features and identity are familiar to the reader because it mirrors reality.

Scholar and literary critic Sabry Hafez writes, 'Mahfouz's literary education was not attained at home where there was no library or literary culture; it was acquired through the popular storytelling of the bard in the coffee-house next to their house.'[1] This fact gives us a glimpse into the relationship between storytelling and a place like the coffeehouse in Mahfouz's coming-of-age experience. As Hafez further remarks:

When Mahfouz went to Cairo University in 1930 he studied philosophy and read avidly. His university years coincided with the economic crisis and political repression of the unstable minority governments in Egypt at that time. The university was a hive of political activity and Mahfouz was a liberal Wafdist – the Wafd was the majority party – working to end British occupation of the country, but he was aware of other political movements, particularly the Leftists and Muslim Brothers, whose exponents appear in many of his novels.[2]

In these novels, including the ones discussed in this chapter, Mahfouz followed a social-realist approach where he used situations and characters drawn from real life while blurring the boundaries between the political, the historical and the fictional. His literature came to dissect the Egyptian urban landscape in the twentieth century, having lived through much of those twentieth-century events he fictionalizes in his literature. His novels and short stories often reflect philosophical and metaphysical notions about the Self, Time, Faith and Love. Literary critic Win-chin Ouyang observes that

> Mahfouz's exclusive devotion to Cairo cannot hide the cosmopolitan outlook underpinning his works. For the city that shaped his thought and literary career was utterly cosmopolitan. Mahfouz never had to travel to acquaint himself with the world; the world came to him through education, translation, work opportunities and intellectual networks.[3]

Moreover, we argue that the Mahfouzian coffeehouse has socio-geographical dimensions which reinforces the elements of diversity and cosmopolitanism in his literature. The location of the traditional *ahwa* or cultural coffeehouse is always a signifier for important happenings whether in the nation or in the life of the characters. *Ahwet Kersha* (Kersha's Café) in *Midaq Alley* (1947), for instance, is located in the centre of the alley, thus reflecting the lifestyle of this traditional, humble neighbourhood of Old Cairo. On the other hand, the coffeeshop of Riri's mistress in *Autumn Quail* (1962) is located by the Corniche in Alexandria to demonstrate a particular cosmopolitan ambience, indicative of the openness in relationships between men and women in the 1950s. Furthermore, El Karnak in his novel *Karnak Café* (1974) is located in downtown Cairo where we see a gallery of modern middle-class characters; while Qushtumur, the coffeehouse where the characters meet in the novel carrying the same title in Arabic but translated into English as *The Coffeehouse* (1988), is in Abbasiyya to signify how this particular suburb has changed over the decades from being an exclusive upper- and upper-middle-class area to a place that is far more inclusive and popular. These coffeehouses also reflect the wide diversity of the social composition of urban life in Egypt, as the following discussion aims to illustrate.

Novelist Gamal al-Ghitani, who was a close friend of Mahfouz, wrote: 'I have never come across anyone more attached to his place of birth than Naguib Mahfouz.'[4] Indeed, the notion of *place* is key to Mahfouz's novels, and it goes hand in hand with the notion of *time*. Al Ghitani further explains that even though Mahfouz's family moved to the Abbasiyya quarter when he was a child, he continued to be attracted to the old neighbourhoods, alleyways, coffeehouses and passageways – to al-Hussein and al-Gamaliyya (where he was born) and to the people whom he knew and who knew him.[5] Al Ghitani tells us in his book *Naguib Mahfouz Yatadhakkar* (Naguib Mahfouz Remembers),[6] which is a compilation of informal interviews and conversations with Mahfouz, that he first met Mahfouz in the early 1960s and went to his literary meetings at the Sphinx coffeehouse, then followed in his footsteps when the meetings moved to Café Riche. In the early 1970s, he joined the weekly Thursday evening meetings with Mahfouz and his friends at the 'Urabi coffeehouse in Abbasiyya. Afterwards, al-Ghitani started meeting up with Mahfouz and his group of friends every Monday in al-Hussein at his favourite coffeehouse, the famous al-Fishawi.[7]

Mahfouz's vast knowledge of the cultural, spatial, temporal and political importance of Cairene coffeehouses is documented in his fiction, which certainly reflects his own interest in them in his private life too. As the coffeehouse was integral to his upbringing and social relationships, he made this strong attachment between his characters and the coffeehouse visible in his fiction. The coffeehouse becomes a place for the production and development of social relations, for bonding and enduring friendships, and also as a sphere where the author could locate his characters to investigate their dispositions, moral systems and trajectories during different historical periods in the twentieth century. Mahfouz himself expressed his attachment to Old Cairo and to al-Gamaliyya in particular in his 'Foreword' to *The Cairo of Naguib Mahfouz*, saying:

> My love and attachment to Old Cairo is unequalled. There are many times when I feel desiccated – experiencing one of those occasional blocks to which writers are prone. Then I take a stroll through old Cairo, and almost immediately I am besieged by a host of images. It is in old Cairo that I have imagined most of my novels. It is there that they have taken place, in my mind before I commit them to paper. And whenever I have felt that an

event or an episode in my writing needs to be anchored in a specific place, al-Gamaliyya has been that place. ... [A]l-Gamaliyya has become a centre, a refuge, and an abode, with its conglomeration of cafés, squares, roads, lanes, and alleys and its ancient mosques and minarets. ... My soul is there always in spite of the passing of long years.[8]

The traditional *ahwa* as a liminal space bearing witness to political and social transformations

In this part, it will become clear that Mahfouz portrayed Old Cairo as a place mirroring the larger Egyptian society, echoing the above quote by the writer. We will examine the notion of *liminal space* and its various signifiers through representations of the *ahwa baladi*. Liminality is perceived here as an 'in-between' or transitional space that the characters temporarily visit before moving on to other social spaces. But while crossing over this liminal space, they go through transformative experiences which mark it as a defining moment in their trajectory and sheds light on new meaning. One of Mahfouz's early novels, which situates the *ahwa* as a liminal space and a place for debating political events as well as engaging in intellectual discussions and forming a bond of fraternity between male friends, is *Khan al-Khalili*, published in 1946.[9] The narrative takes place during the Second World War, specifically the year 1941–2, when Cairo suffered repeated raids and bombshells as a result of the presence of the British colonial force and Britain's involvement in the war. We also read in the novel about the summer of 1942 and the German troops' advent to al-Alamein in the Egyptian western desert under Rommel's leadership, and the anticipation of Egyptians that the Axis powers would defeat the Allies and advance into Alexandria. Of course this did not happen because Rommel's army failed in the famous battle of al-Alamein and retreated.

Thus, the novel's events take place against this historical backdrop where the characters from different social and educational backgrounds get to know each other as residents of the Khan al-Khalili neighbourhood, the heart of Islamic Cairo, where two revered mosques are located: al-Azhar and al-Hussein. We first encounter Ahmed Akef, the main protagonist, who has just moved with his parents from the high-class suburb of Sakakini to the more popular (*sha'bi*) neighbourhood of Khan al-Khalili, the reason being that Sakakini was brutally hit by violent raids and Akef's family home was damaged. Hence, the family begins to experience a different lifestyle once they move to the Khan: the hustle and bustle of the alleyways, crowdedness and street noise, close ties between the neighbours, and a far more diverse and vibrant social environment. Akef visits *ahwet al-Zahra* (Zahra Café) where he begins to spend the evenings with a few of his male neighbours.

It is at the Zahra Café where Akef, 40 years of age, a civil servant at a government ministry, and introduced to the reader as an introverted and solitary individual, starts gradually to become a sociable and loveable person among the neighbours. He is on the threshold of a new and exciting experience at this liminal space. He gets to know the residents of the Khan by frequenting the café every evening; and more importantly he starts to become at peace with his inner feelings through this newly established social network. The neighbours of course experience one thing in common: the war and political uncertainty and having to stay in the underground shelters during the hours of the night raids. While the café is frequented only by men, the shelter is where everybody (women, men and children) find themselves together, side by side, trying to feel some comfort and courage collectively. In the shelter, liminality is further reinforced to signify the situation of 'waiting' and 'transition' that these people go through during the raids.

However, the Khan does not only include the Zahra Café, but many others as Akef finds out. He ponders that there must be 'one café for every ten men in the Khan'.[10] He begins to get used to the new neighbourhood, and the café comes to symbolize a 'refuge' for his lost soul. We read that he was never married, has no close friends and is only interested in reading books. Indeed, the reader witnesses Akef's character development as a result of becoming part of this new group of friends at the café, where each man is free to express himself the way he desires. Even though at the start Akef thinks of them as 'amusing and strange types of people',[11] he gradually grows fond of them, and frequenting the café becomes a daily habit. His new friends drag him away from his existential sense of social isolation and angst.

At the café, we meet Mo'allim Nunu who is married to four wives and has many children; Ahmed Rashed, a lawyer and socialist; Kamal Khalil, another civil servant and Akef's next-door neighbour whom the latter falls in love with his 16-year old daughter; and the café owner Mo'allim Shiffah who smokes dope all the time; among others. Hence, the café's characters come to mirror many ideas about patriarchy and social relations in the Egyptian society at the time: men have the upper hand in the household and they can have more than one wife if they so desire; women are not permitted into the outdoor social gatherings but only indoors when they visit each other at home; smoking hashish and having extra-marital relations are common among men of various age groups and social backgrounds; and the public space is intensely inhabited by men far more than women. Those women who mix with men in their gatherings or host them at their houses while smoking and drinking with them are perceived as prostitutes, similar to 'Aliyyat in the novel.

Throughout the narrative, we get the sense that Mahfouz is not only shedding light on social and gender relations at a time of critical political transition in Egypt, but is actually portraying to us minute details of this magnanimous and unique place in the heart of Islamic Cairo: Khan al-Khalili. There is much emphasis on how people go about their daily livelihoods, but also how they celebrate collectively during special occasions such as the fasting month of Ramadan and the Islamic feasts. It is through details about these socially vibrant events – the food that people prepare for each occasion, how they dress, their hairstyles and the living rooms where they gather and socialize – that the notion of *place* and its function in Mahfouz's narrative is illuminated. The place and its people convey to us a broad range of emotions and sentiments; hence we begin to see these characters as portraits reflecting a specific society.

At the Zahra Café, we encounter revealing conversations between the characters, their philosophical reflections about the war, the colonial regime and the passage of time (getting married, becoming older, seeing the children grow up, etc.). These are some trademarks of Mahfouz's images of the coffeehouse in his different narratives. The characters are always on the verge of crossing over the threshold to experience something new, but not necessarily a favourable one. In the reader's mind, the Zahra Café perhaps comes to resemble a theatre stage where each character takes his turn to express his ideas and inner feelings, but then each voice is part of a greater collective where they also have a conversation and listen to each other, laugh, joke and bond. Many of these ideas expressed at the café are in fact reactionary, biased (especially against women) and misogynistic; yet the aim is to show a gendered picture of the larger society with its different types of people at a particular period of time. The liminal space of the café allows Mahfouz to unpack taboo issues which the male characters might not express in other spaces such as the home or the workplace.

For the protagonist Ahmed Akef, the Zahra Café becomes like a second home where he tries to overcome his sorrows during the tragic illness of his much loved brother Rushdi, as well as his failed love life. But at the end of the novel, Akef will have to leave the neighbourhood which grew very close to his heart. This lively neighbourhood which brought joy to Akef's life has transformed into a 'cursed' place which witnessed the untimely death of his younger brother. The last line in the novel reads: 'Farewell Khan al-Khalili'.[12] This accentuates the point that the place as a whole was a transitional period in his life.

Whereas this novel recreates a well-known traditional quarter of a city going through political turmoil and identity crisis in the midst of a war situation, Mahfouz's next novel, *Zoqaq al-Madaq* (*Midaq Alley*), published in 1947,[13] zooms into a small alley (a real one), *a detail* in the larger canvas of Islamic Cairo. Through fictionalizing the alley's characters' way of life, the author delves into the underbelly of the city, characterized by illicit relationships, crimes, drug dealings and hidden desires. Similar to Aslan's *The Heron*, albeit situated in an earlier period, *Midaq Alley* also captures the image of 'subaltern' characters who reflect Asef Bayat's concept of the city-inside-out: 'In the city-inside-out, the subaltern are seen and felt to be almost everywhere. In fact they are everywhere.'[14] Interestingly, the subaltern in Mahfouz's novel are also colonized subjects. But contrary to Gayatri Spivak's argument in her essay 'Can the Subaltern Speak?'[15] that the colonized, especially impoverished women, do not have the agency to speak for themselves, Mahfouz's characters do speak loudly and noisily, thus asserting their agency and right to public space.

The location of Midaq alley is concealed from the main road leading to al-Azhar; and what happens there is also concealed from the public eye, in a stark contrast to a place like Khan al-Khalili where everything is clear and visible. And in that small alley, a place almost forgotten and abandoned by modernity where electricity has not even reached its homes, a place insignificant and unknown, the central location which constitutes its pulse is the liminal space of *ahwet Kersha* (Kersha's Café).[16] Mahfouz brings this extremely peripheral alley with its café and marginalized subjects to the centre of the readers and critics' attention. The *real* Midaq Alley did gain notoriety and fame since the publication of Mahfouz's novel especially after it was adapted to cinema.[17]

Similar to Mahfouz's earlier novel *Khan al-Khalili*, the events of *Midaq Alley* take place during the Second World War, specifically in its final year. However, the characters do not know that the war is about to end. We learn that two of the alley's young men, Abbas el-Helw and Hussein Kersha, are working at the British army camps because they get paid well. El Helw has decided to leave behind his barbershop to follow in the footsteps of his friend Hussein who was already working for the British, in order to make some money and marry his sweetheart Hamida. At Kersha's Café, we get introduced to the key characters of the novel who are from different age groups and social classes. Among them are wealthy merchants such as Selim 'Ulwan and others who are impoverished and homeless such as Sheikh Darwish. Through their collectivity and diversity, these characters point to the social composition of the alley: a humble place where the neighbours know each other and form a strong network of interests and relations. Yet some of its young people like Hamida and Hussein aspire to leave it and move on to live outside, in the bigger city. They want to climb the social ladder, be part of the modern world and become rich. Once again, these characters want to cross over the threshold to another state of being.

Mahfouz situates Kersha's Café at the heart of the alley where the men who frequent it throughout the day and night exchange news about their neighbours and the war situation. The café is their entertainment centre and this is accentuated in the opening chapter when we learn that the café owner has bought a second-hand radio to install there, which was a novelty at the time. Thus, the men gather in the evening around the gas lamps to listen to the radio, play cards, have hot drinks, talk about politics and smoke dope. They are together in this small café, the 'in-between' place, but their eyes are focused on what is taking place beyond them outside in the larger city. Here, we see 'types' of characters who resemble many others in similar locations in Cairo. But the social background of the café's visitors is different from those whom we have encountered at the Zahra Café in *Khan al-Khalili*. Most of the characters in *Midaq Alley* belong to the poor, illiterate strata of the city who are barely able to make ends meet. However, we also encounter a small number of characters who run their own businesses or own property, hence they are wealthy but have chosen to stay in the alley. Mo'allim Kersha himself, the café owner, would not leave the alley although his financial means allow him to do so, and despite the fact that his 'scandals' and homosexual affairs are well-known to everyone. In this way, although extremely peripheral as a place, most of the older characters consider the alley their home and would not leave it for any other place.

In the Egyptian cultural imaginary, Kersha's Café of Midaq Alley is perceived as one of the most popular portrayals of a traditional *ahwa baladi* in Egyptian literature and cinema, because it is here that we see depicted an archetypal café in a strictly Egyptian style. As mentioned earlier, the café resembles a 'character' in its own right, standing as a witness to social and political transformations, as well as the trajectories of the characters. The café's doors are always open to both friends and strangers who might be passing by the alley. When the women open their *mashrabiyyas* (or wooden shutters), the first thing they see is the café and they can follow what the men are up to. The masculine, strictly male society of the café is set in contrast to the exclusive women's quarters, mainly their homes. Yet, the women of the alley are strong characters and far from being submissive or weak, such as Umm Hamida, Umm Hussein (Kersha's wife) and Hosniyya who runs a small bakery shop.

But for a beautiful, young woman like Hamida – poor, orphaned and illiterate – her utmost ambition is to leave the alley and marry a rich man: 'She worships money as it's the magical key to life and its luxuries.'[18] From the start of the novel, we are made aware of Hamida's passionate yearning for independence, reminding herself every now and then that she grew up without a mother or a father. Although she was adopted by one of the alley's women whose title accordingly became Umm Hamida (Hamida's mother), Hamida could not develop any strong bond with the alley and its inhabitants. Rather, her eyes are fixed on the men, aiming to find a prospective suitor, but the only one who has fallen for her is Abbas. In Hamida's eyes, Abbas is a good person but poor. He will not be able to satisfy her material ambitions: 'She dreamt of money; money which buys clothes and everything that one desires.'[19] Even though they get engaged, she does not stop searching for a wealthy man. And it is through Kersha's Café that she begins to notice Farag Ibrahim, a pimp and an outsider to the alley, who has decided to frequent the café so he could recruit Hamida. He has met her by a mere chance, and now he is determined to dazzle her with the prospect of becoming a rich woman. Farag runs a number of brothels and nightclubs to entertain the foreign soldiers during the war. Finally, Hamida leaves the alley and elopes with him, falling into prostitution. She crosses over the threshold to a new, but dangerous, life.

Throughout the narrative, Mahfouz is juxtaposing material gain alongside morals while testing his characters and putting them in difficult situations where they have to choose between the two, especially during a time of political and economic uncertainty. By anchoring the main protagonists' lives, particularly Hamida and Hussein, around these two axes, Mahfouz is also reflecting on how individuals can fall into the trap of greed, which would consequently lead to their demise. Hamida ends up as a sex worker in the hands of Farag Ibrahim, and Hussein ends up unemployed and poor after he was expelled from the British camps. When Abbas discovers what has befallen Hamida, seeing her in the company of British soldiers in a nightclub, he attacks her which eventually leads to his murder at the hands of the drunken soldiers.

But Mahfouz's novel is not meant to be a moral tale. He situates the characters in a way to shed light on a particular period in Egypt's history when a place like Midaq Alley was symbolic of transitions in social relations as a result of the war situation and the presence of the British colonial regime. Towards the end of the novel, the emphasis is on Kersha's Café that continues to bear witness to all these happenings in the alley. The characters come and go, leave or stay, die or go to prison, but the alley remains, forgetting sometimes those who have died or departed. Literary critic Sabry Hafez makes this key observation about Mahfouz's novels during the decade of the 1940s, including *Khan al-Khalili* and *Midaq Alley*:

> The novels of this phase ... reflect the trauma of change and its social, human and political consequences. They shift the focus of the Arabic novel from the country to the city, from the past to the present; they force it to deal with the problems of change and the conflict between the old and the new, between tradition and modernity.[20]

Another novel by Mahfouz where the traditional *ahwa* stands as a liminal space witnessing political and social changes in Cairo, as well as a signifier for identity formations, is *al-Sukkariyya* (*Sugar Street*), the third volume of the *Cairo Trilogy*, published in 1957.[21] Indeed, this trope of tradition versus modernity, mentioned in Hafez's quote above, carries on in the *Trilogy* while reaching a crisis point in the third part. Al Sukkariyya is an actual street name in al-Gamaliyya district, not far from Khan al-Khalili. This third volume of the famous *Trilogy* (the first two being *Palace Walk* and *Palace of Desire*) focuses on the third generation of al-Sayyed Ahmed Abdel Gawwad's family or his grandchildren whose house is located in al-Sukkariyya, specifically during the years 1935–44 when Egypt was going through many decisive political battles between the Wafd party, the Palace and the British colonial regime. It is also the period which witnessed the rise of the Wafd leader Mustapha al-Nahhas as the 'people's leader', and then his demise after failing to force the British to grant Egypt its independence. The novel concludes in 1944 just before the war ends, when two of al-Sayyed's grandchildren are taken to prison (in a mass arrest of opposition activists) due to their anti-government political activities: one was a communist and the other a Muslim Brother.

Here, we also see how Abdel Gawwad's youngest son Kamal has grown into a mature man, working as a primary school teacher and a freelance writer. Kamal is not much older than his nephews, so they more or less belong to the same generation. The nephews come to look at their uncle as a source of respect and inspiration. Yet, Kamal himself is still wandering aimlessly in his inner world of philosophical reflections, self-doubt and great uncertainty about the future. He has rejected the idea of marriage after his first failed love affair and has decided to devote his free time to writing philosophical articles (which very few people can understand) in the elitist *al-Fikr* magazine for the intelligentsia class.

But Kamal has a passion for discussions about world affairs and philosophy (echoing Mahfouz himself), hence he meets with his two friends Ismail and Riad in Ahmad Abduh coffeehouse, an old *ahwa baladi* built under the ground.[22] We were introduced to this coffeehouse in the first two parts of the *Trilogy*. In fact, Kamal is a lover of coffee as the daily 'coffee hour' at his family home was an integral part of his upbringing. Amina, his mother, would gather her children in the late afternoon to drink coffee together and tell stories, before the strict father and patriarch of the household, al-Sayyed Ahmed, comes back from work; thus 'a democratic matriarchal interaction replaces the oppressive patriarchal order.'[23] Throughout the *Trilogy*, Mahfouz makes this daily coffee gathering between Amina and her children imprinted in the reader's mind. It was her main outlet from the daily chores and the rigid rules of her husband.

Thus, we read in *al-Sukkariyya* how Kamal is well acquainted with Ahmad Abduh coffeehouse. He has grown so attached to it because he perceives it as a remnant of past times, or (*athar*) as he calls it. When the news reaches him that the coffeehouse would be demolished and a new apartment block would take its place, Kamal's sense of melancholy and disappointment grows deeper:

> My dear coffeehouse, you're part of me. I have dreamt a lot and thought a lot inside you. Yassin[24] came to you for years. Fahmy[25] met his revolutionary comrades here to plan for a better world. I also love you, because you are made from the same stuff as dreams. But what's the use of all this? What value does nostalgia have?[26]

Sitting in the coffeehouse, sheltered by its walls, Kamal reminisces about his past memories and the above inner monologue encapsulates how he personifies the place as a 'being' that witnessed his coming-of-age experience. Indeed, the coffeehouse's location under the ground made it possible for students' demonstrations against the British or the king to start from its doors then move onto the larger roads. It is where diverse political debates have taken place. For example, we see in the novel how Kamal's nephews, the brothers Abdel Mon'eim and Ahmed, also frequent the coffeehouse, while the former sits with the newly formed Muslim Brotherhood group to listen to religious lessons in the early 1930s. Abdel Mon'eim later becomes a member of the group whereas his brother becomes a communist.

Ahmad Abduh coffeehouse is also portrayed as a place which has seen different generations of young men coming and going, discussing politics and world affairs, and shaping their political identity as they grow into manhood. Thus, the coffeehouse's liminality is underscored as an 'in-between' place where Kamal crosses over from the past to the unknown future of his country. But a place like this will have to disappear as Cairo is transforming into a modern city and apartment blocks are replacing the old traditional shops and houses. Eventually, we learn that the coffeehouse has been demolished. However, Mahfouz charts for us a brief *map* of other cafés in al-Hussein and al-Azhar areas to show their various functions and also their increasing number in that part of the city. For example, Kamal's eldest brother Yassin frequents al-ʿAtaba Café because he can have cheaper drinks there, and can also gaze at the women passers-by from the window and flirt with them. After the disappearance of Ahmad Abduh coffeehouse, Kamal moved to al-Hussein Café; and during the war he and his friends would hide in the shelter of Rex Café from the violent raids and bomb shelling. Towards the end of the novel, we learn that a new café called Khan al-Khalili has been built (above the ground) to replace the old Ahmad Abduh coffeehouse, and it has become the favourite meeting place for Kamal and his friends.

In this way, Mahfouz points to how the traditional cafés were part and parcel of the social and political life of Old Cairo at the time, exclusively for men's gatherings or as hideouts. Through the men's conversations and continuous political discussions, the reader gets to know about the changing political landscape in Egypt in the years leading up to the Second World War and the aftermath.

As we have argued so far, the traditional *ahwa* has spatial and social implications in Mahfouz's works: its location and the social status of the characters who frequent it point to its function and the type of service it provides. In another iconic novel by Mahfouz, *al-Summan wal Kharif* (*Autumn Quail*), published in 1962,[27] we follow the trajectory of the protagonist Isa al-Dabbagh, a high-profile civil servant before the 1952 revolution, who was pensioned off after the revolution as he was implicated in bribery during his time in office. He is presented to the Purge Committee and consequently loses his job. The novel opens with the Cairo Fire in January 1952 and concludes in 1956 shortly after the Suez War.

As Isa is unable to be part of the new regime, his feelings as an 'outsider' intensify. He travels between Cairo and Alexandria, and we see how he meets with his friends and acquaintances in several coffeehouses throughout the narrative, where gradually the coffeehouse becomes a refuge for him or a liminal space that traces his transition from one state of mind to another. As we follow in his footsteps, we encounter some of the famous coffeehouses where middle- and upper-class Egyptians used to frequent in the 1950s such as Athineos and Trianon in Alexandria,[28] and the Bodega and Groppi in Cairo. The Bodega becomes Isa's favourite coffeehouse where he can hide from the outside world and would only meet his close friends.

However, Mahfouz presents another significant storyline in the novel, around Riri's character. Riri, the Alexandrian sex worker whom Isa meets in one of his visits to the city, transforms from a poor, helpless and homeless young woman at the start of the narrative to a strong, empowered woman later on. When Isa first meets Riri by a mere chance, she asks him if she could stay at his flat because she did not have a place to sleep, except the café of her mistress. Isa agrees to let Riri stay and their relationship develops to the point that Riri gets pregnant. But Isa is not willing to marry her, so he behaves aggressively and kicks her out of his flat. He rejects all her pleas and insists on banishing her completely from his life. We do not read about Riri again until the last chapters of the novel, four years later, when Isa encounters her by coincidence in a small shop for selling sandwiches and soft drinks by the Corniche in Alexandria. He also sees a female child with her, and it immediately strikes him that this child must be his own daughter.

Isa spends hours watching Riri, not able to understand her role in the shop, until he asks one of the workers in the area about her, only to learn that she is the manageress of the shop. Her husband is in prison and has left the shop for her to run. This news bewilders Isa as he suddenly begins to consider Riri in a new light. It is his turn now to plea with her so he could stay with her and his daughter. But Riri rejects him and does not even acknowledge his presence. She has banished him from her life as well, as he had done to her years earlier. Riri has been empowered as a mother and as a businesswoman.

In *Autumn Quail*, the representation of the coffeehouse takes a different dimension, as now Mahfouz is portraying the 1950s' modern Egyptian city, whether Cairo or Alexandria. The stylish coffeehouse is a social space for the affluent, yet the traditional *ahwa baladi* is still prominent in the cities. One signifier of the gap between Isa and Riri in social status is indeed the type of coffeeshop each of them frequents. But here, we are also introduced to a female manageress of an *ahwa* (Riri's mistress), a new development in the modern city, as the *ahwa* used to be exclusively a male domain as we have seen in Mahfouz's earlier novels.

In this way, through imagining the *ahwa* as a liminal space in his characters' lives, Mahfouz was able to show the complex transformations of gender and class relations during times of critical political change in urban Egypt. Building on these images, we will focus in the next part on two of Mahfouz's works, namely *Karnak Café* and *The Coffeehouse*, where the coffeehouse comes to play a more significant role as a literary metaphor for the society as a whole.

The coffeehouse as a microcosm of the larger society

In Mahfouz's novella *El Karnak* (*Karnak Café*), published in 1974,[29] we read about *ahwet el Karnak*, owned by the beautiful manageress Qurunfula (a former belly dancer). At this coffeehouse, all the main characters get together to discuss political issues, expand their social networks and speak freely about their ideas in art, culture and politics. Through Mahfouz's representation, the reader feels that this particular coffeehouse mirrors the real Café Riche on Talaat Harb Street. Karnak Café, similar to Riche, reflects a secular space located in a modern, cosmopolitan quarter of Cairo, starkly different from the setting in Old Cairo in Mahfouz's earlier novels.

Karnak Café opens with a chapter entitled 'Qurunfula', thus underscoring the portrait of a female café owner. From the outset, the anonymous narrator draws our attention to both the coffeehouse and its owner, suggesting that their trajectories are intertwined. In the first few lines, he provides this description:

> It was sheer chance that brought me to Karnak Café. ... It's very small and off the main street. Since that day it's become my favorite place to sit and pass the time. To tell you the truth, at first I hesitated by the entrance for a moment, but then I spotted a woman sitting on a stool by the cash register, the usual spot for the manageress. You could tell she was getting old, and yet she still had vestiges of her former beauty. Those clear, refined features of hers jogged something buried deep in my memory. ... A dancer, that's what she was. Yes, the star of 'Imad al-Din', none other than Qurunfula herself. Now there she was sitting at the stool, Qurunfula in person, the roseate dream from the 1940s. So that was how I came to enter the Karnak Café. I felt drawn in by some obscure magic force and a carefree heart.[30]

Through the detailed description by the narrator, we begin to formulate a visual image of Qurunfula and that she is well respected and highly regarded by all her customers. The novella's events begin around the year 1965 and continue until after the 1967 June War defeat, as the narrator reveals to us details about the customers who come from different age groups and educational backgrounds. There is the older generation, a group of retired men who frequent the coffeehouse and have befriended Qurunfula; and there is the younger generation, a group of university students who also hang out at the coffeehouse and enliven the place with their discussions and unconventional ideas. Among them are the protagonists Hilmi Hamada, Ismail al-Sheikh and Zeinab Diab. The latter two are from the same neighbourhood, the working-class al-Husseiniyya quarter. They grew up together and were engaged to be married.

Yet, the café is also inhabited by spies and *mukhbireen* (informers), although they are discreet and unknown to Qurunfula or the other customers. These informers eventually lead to the arrest and torture of the university students, who were suspected to be involved in underground political activity against the regime. This period in Egypt's history witnessed the height of Gamal Abdel Nasser's 'Secret Police State', and it is mostly the university students who were watched and reported upon over the course of the novella. The work is overtly political where Mahfouz directs a sharp critique against the corruption and brutality of the Intelligence and Secret Police apparatuses under the Nasser regime.

Even though the characters we meet at Karnak Café are different from one another, the narrator reveals that they all support the 1952 revolution, hence the implication that they support Nasser's state as well. He refers to the students as 'the children of the revolution'.[31] We also learn that Qurunfula is in love with one of the students, Hilmi, although he is much younger than her. The narrator develops an insight into the café's dynamics and befriends the other customers, and more importantly Qurunfula. The reader is exposed to many details about the characters through the narrator's lens and his conversations with the main protagonists.

But things take a sharp turn when unexpectedly the students disappear for weeks and they stop coming to the coffeehouse. Qurunfula, together with the narrator, could not find an explanation for their absence except when some of the customers start talking about the wide arrests of many students. But the narrator says in response that those students who frequent the coffeehouse are strong supporters of the 1952 revolution, so why would they be arrested? Qurunfula falls to pieces worrying about her lover Hilmi. However, the students come back after a few weeks but only to disappear again, and then again (three times within two years).

The narrator conveys to us that during their third absence, the war erupts. It is June 1967 and the whole country is in turmoil. No one knows what has happened to the students. Political debates take centre stage at the café about the war defeat and its consequences on Egypt and the whole Arab world. The atmosphere grows bleak and ambiguous. After the war, the students reappear at the café but without Hilmi, who is believed to have been tortured to death in detention.

The narrator concludes the first part by stating that his friendship grew over time with Ismail al-Sheikh and Zeinab Diab, and they both revealed to him the missing details about their relationship and imprisonment. The following three parts are entitled 'Ismail al-Sheikh', 'Zeinab Diab' and 'Khalid Safwan' (the latter is the brutal intelligence officer who masterminded the kidnapping and torture of the students). Through conversations between the narrator and the two students, Mahfouz exposes the horrors of political detention at the time and the irreversible physical and psychological damage which this entailed. By juxtaposing the character of Khalid Safwan to Zeinab and Ismail, Mahfouz is suggesting a complex relationship between the victim and victimizer for the reader to consider them side by side.

In the last short chapter entitled 'Khalid Safwan', the narrator describes the atmosphere at the café in the few years following the *naksa* (setback) or the 1967 war defeat. The customers are occupied with one primary theme: when will the next war erupt with the enemy? The narrator says that their discussions have focused on this topic over and again until one day everyone is bewildered by the appearance of Khalid Safwan himself at the café. Safwan makes a public come back after spending three years in prison and the confiscation of his property. He comes across as a feeble, sick man, yet he makes his voice heard to the customers. He reappears at the café several times as if haunting the other characters and reminding them of the past. Then, one day he leaves and never comes back. With Safwan's departure from the scene, Mahfouz concludes his novella with the rise of a new young member at the café, Mounir, whom the narrator feels that he represents a new hope in the long bleak tunnel the country was in.

Thus, Mahfouz here uses al-Karnak Café as a space to reflect on the state of political instability, confusion and violence which Egypt was entangled in before and after June 1967. The café serves as a microcosm of the relationship between the state apparatus with its visible force, and ordinary citizens whose terrible fate has brought them under the brutal arm of the regime through the mere chance of frequenting a café. By following the students' trajectories through critique and commentary, Mahfouz is able to dissect the society's 'malaise' while suggesting that even those who were not involved in politics – ordinary people like Zeinab and Ismail – could find themselves as direct victims of such a senseless, irrational police and intelligence order.

There is certainly an element of tragic irony in this representation, but the fact is that Mahfouz's story mirrored what was happening in Egypt during those years and thereafter. Since then, there have been times when thousands of young political activists were kidnapped from cafés and disappeared, imprisoned, tortured or murdered. Literary critic Trevor LeGassick considers Karnak Café as a metaphor for Egypt at the time. He observes that the novella's 'graphic portrayal of the excesses of the repressive machinery of Nasir's police state was a shocking revelation to many Egyptians'.[32]

While *Karnak Café* focuses on a particular period of Egypt's history in the late 1960s and early 1970s, in *Qushtumur*, a later novel by Mahfouz published in 1988,[33] or *The Coffeehouse* in the English translation (2010), the novelist charts seven decades of the country's history by following a group of friends who have witnessed many key political events during those seven decades (1910–85). As the anonymous narrator tells us, Qushtumur is the name of a coffeehouse located between the Dhaher and Abbasiyya suburbs in Cairo.[34] It becomes the place where the five protagonist friends meet on a daily basis to discuss many subjects related to their lives. We follow the trajectories of Sadiq, Ismail, Hamada and Taher through the lens of the anonymous narrator who is the fifth friend in the group. However, he is a mere 'storyteller', and we do not get to know any details about his own life. He plays the role of the 'commentator' or the 'reliable narrator'.

Once again, in this novel, the coffeehouse stands as a witness to the development of the four characters and their coming-of-age experiences in education, sexual relations, politics, love and religion. Qushtumur comes to reflect a microcosm of Egyptian society over most of the twentieth century. The narrator/friend sets the scene of the narrative from the first passage by describing Abbasiyya:

> Abbasiyya in its lost youth. An oasis in the heart of a vast desert. In its east loomed mansions like little fortresses, and in its west were small, clustered houses, vain of their hidden gardens and of their newness. On more than one side it was enfolded by green fields, and by forests of date palms, henna plants, and prickly pear trees. Its calm and quiet would have been complete but for the humming of the white tram, shuttling on its well-worn tracks between suburban Heliopolis and Ataba Square. The dry desert wind that beat down, drawing the deepest perfumes from the field, stirred secret love in the breasts of men. And just at sunset, the *rabab* player, wrapped in his long *galabiyya*, meandered through the street, bare-footed and goggle-eyed, chanting in a rasping voice, but not without a piercing air:

> *I put my trust in you, O Time,*
> *But you returned to betray me.*[35]

Mahfouz draws a picture of the place, detailing its past beauty and peaceful ambience but also how the rich and the poor lived side by side. It is the place where the memories and recollections of the four protagonists are centred around. The reader will follow with them how Abbasiyya, and in turn Cairo, changed over seven decades.

The narrator then goes on to give us some biographical details about this group of friends: they were all born in 1910, went to the same primary school when they were 5 years old and left it when they were 9. Hence they met in 1915, and since then they never left their suburb, Abbasiyya. Even though they had many other friends in their group, the core of five stayed together throughout the good and bad days; and even the gap in social status did not separate them over the decades. Ismail and Sadiq were from west Abbasiyya (the poorer quarter); Hamada lived in a mansion while Taher lived in a huge villa in east Abbasiyya (the wealthy quarter). Yet, 'the five are one and the one is five', as the narrator states.[36] He adds: 'Our luck and our destinies have changed over time, but Abbasiyya is still our home and Qushtumur still our coffeehouse. Its corners have echoed with our chatter, our laughter, and our tears – and the sound of our heartbeats that have pulsed without end in the beating breast of Cairo.'[37]

In this way, it is suggested from the outset that the five friends are social and cultural products of the place they have lived in. Mahfouz situates them in the coffeehouse which is located in a particular suburb that has certain geographical and social characteristics, which is in turn part of the big city. In the reader's imagination, this setting could resemble a multilayered structure or perhaps a labyrinth. We are about to hear the stories of these friends as they reminisce and recollect their memories, going through a chain of dates, events, and historical and political happenings where the fictional intersects with the real. Over the course of the narrative, we realize that Qushtumur is not any café, but one with specific characteristics, the most important of which is its continuity during all these decades. As the narrator reflects towards the end of the novel, 'Our corner in Qushtumur remains. May God keep it forever! It is the only stable place in our lives, no matter what other storms around us occur.'[38]

The protagonists get to know about this coffeehouse in their first year in secondary school, when they were only 13 years old. The narrator describes the place as a small, beautiful coffeehouse, with a little garden at the back, and mirrors inside. The five friends choose their corner there to play backgammon and drink tea; and this is where they will meet every evening for the next 60 years. They became the 'landmark' of the place;[39] and Qushtumur 'endured as if it is a second country for us';[40] 'Qushtumur witnessed our passing youth and as we were entering maturity.'[41] It is enormously indicative here that they refer to the coffeehouse as their second *country* rather than a second *home*. The place was part of their identity, and they in turn shaped its trajectory as the years went by. When they decided to celebrate the seventieth year of their friendship in 1985, they could not have the party at any other place but in Qushtumur: 'We look at an old photo and we compare, in bewilderment, how we were and how we have become; and we get closer and more fond of each other. And Qushtumur is like one of our bodily organs.'[42] They have grown old, as did the coffeehouse.

Over these seven decades, the reader follows the impact of key political events on the lives of the five protagonists, passing through the 1919 revolution and their first awareness of the national question and the British colonial regime; how they believed in the leader Sa'd Zaghloul from whom they learned a strong sense of belonging to the nation; how they witnessed the rise of the Wafd party and their friend Ismail's attachment to it (more so than the other members of the group); then the death of Saʻd in 1927 and the Wafd crisis in the mid-1930s; life under the hardships of the Second World War; the 1952 revolution and the rise of the Free Officers' regime and how this impacted on their friend Hamada's family in particular because they lost much of their property during the nationalization years; then the disaster of the 1967 war defeat and the ensuing fall from grace of Gamal Abdel Nasser, his death and the rise of Anwar Sadat to power; the new economic era of *infitah* (open-door policy) and the expansion of corruption and money laundering which permeated the country; and finally Sadat's assassination and the rise of a new president to power. Yet, these historical events acquire more significance when we read about their influence on peoples' lives like the four protagonists and how their livelihoods, jobs, wealth, marriages, households and so on changed as a result of these events. Perhaps this is the most significant aspect of Mahfouz's novel, to show history and politics from a multiplicity of viewpoints of the individuals who were affected by them as well as how these people also took part in these events through their political activism, writings and business operations.

Alongside such immense political changes, Abbasiyya (and in turn Cairo) has also transformed dramatically. The narrator interrupts the narrative from time to time to relay how Abbasiyya itself was changing from a quiet, leafy, residential suburb to a sort of a 'city' within the bigger city, characterized by noise and traffic; the disappearance of the mansions, villas and green fields to be replaced by cement and steel apartment blocks to the extent that there was no longer a social gap between its east and west quarters; the quick spread of shops on its quiet streets and the increasing crowdedness as more people have moved to live there. However, the most significant impact was during the Second World War years when the British troops established their barracks in Abbasiyya, hence changing the function and architecture of the place forever. Yet, the five friends would not leave to live anywhere else. In the final pages of the novel, the narrator reflects on how the past has come to be the only source of 'pleasure' and 'magic' for his group of friends, as Qushtumur continues to shelter them from the uncertainties of the present.

Interestingly, this is one of very few novels by Mahfouz which focuses primarily on male characters. We get to know about the female characters through the men's eyes. Qushtumur is certainly a 'hyper-masculine' setting which raises questions as to why the novelist was following this approach in a later work in his life. The novel feels like a story of the past, chronicling the life of Mahfouz's own generation, and perhaps the author himself identified on a personal level with the trajectories of the five friends.

Conclusion

This chapter has attempted to examine a selection of novels by Naguib Mahfouz to explore the extent to which his literature has offered a realistic and relatable picture of the coffeehouse in the life of Egyptians. He is read here as the 'storyteller' of coffeehouses. His novels show how frequenting the coffeehouse is an everyday Egyptian social practice which sheds much light on notions of belonging and identity formations within various communities and during different historical periods of the twentieth century. The literature we have discussed here underscores the notion of the *ahwa* as a 'liminal space' in the life of the characters, as a 'microcosm' of the larger society, and as a 'second home' if not *the* home (or even *the* country) for some characters.

Through the analysis in Chapters 3 and 4, we can see clearly how Egyptian writers have used the coffeehouse as a setting and a metaphor to investigate political, economic and social changes taking place in the country throughout the twentieth century. This social space has also helped them to follow the trajectories of their multilayered characters. One essential and unique feature of the coffeehouse is that it embodies male characters who tell stories about their lives, hence reflecting gender and class relations in their communities and by extension within the country as a whole. The coffeehouse mirrors Egyptian society with its complex relations between rich and poor, men and women, religious and non-religious, and old and young.

In the next chapter, we will move on to another cultural genre and consider the cinematic field to analyse the representation of the coffeehouse in a selection of popular films from different periods, trace their cultural and spatial implications and discuss their visual aesthetics. Through our examination of these films, we will focus on gender and class issues as manifested in Egyptian society during various historical eras.

5

Multilayered representations of the coffeehouse in Egyptian cinema

Introduction: The symbiotic relation between *ahwa*, cinema and urban space

Similar to its immense presence in literary works as we have examined in Chapters 3 and 4, the *ahwa baladi* figures in a vast array of Egyptian films from the 1940s onwards. Interestingly, in the overwhelming majority of these films, the traditional café has been situated in urban space especially the big cities of Cairo and Alexandria. This is extremely significant as an indication of the centrality of this social space in the city life of Egyptians in the past and present, and reinforces its presence in literary representations. Cinema is one of the most popular cultural media in Egypt, and the Egyptian *national* film industry has been the largest in the Arab world since the inception of film-making in the early part of the twentieth century during the colonial era.[1] Historically, many films have been adapted from literary works, and this has proved most effective in engaging the general public with classical and modern fiction by established Egyptian authors such as Mohammad Hussein Haikal, Tawfiq al-Hakim, Yehia Haqqi, Youssef Idris, Latifa al-Zayyat, Ihsan Abdel Quddous and Naguib Mahfouz.[2]

Cinema was the product of both Egyptian and foreign artists inhabiting Cairo and Alexandria. The first movie theatre opened in Alexandria in 1897, and the first in Cairo opened in 1906.[3] These early movie theatres were owned by foreigners or by European immigrants (particularly Italians) who lived in Egypt.[4] Initially, film production was confined to non-Egyptian investors, but starting from 1928, two films on average were produced annually thus attracting Egyptian producers, actors and directors (e.g. Aziza Amir, Fatema

Rushdi, Naguib al-Rihani, Youssef Wahbi and director Mohammad Karim),[5] the pioneers who contributed to the cultural economy of the cities.

The theme of the relationship between cinema and space has attracted numerous theorists and film scholars in Europe and the United States to explore this rich field in the history of film-making. But this subject area is extremely lagging behind in academic research and critical analysis where Arab and Egyptian cinemas are concerned. Therefore, this chapter aims to explore the cultural and political implications of the traditional café (*ahwa baladi*) as a 'concrete place' imagined and visualized as part of urban space by Egyptian film-makers from different eras. We will investigate the deep-seated relationship between Egyptian cinema and urban space and the location of the café within it as a significant field of inquiry. The focus is specifically on the traditional café as it is the place that is most represented in cinematic production, rather than the cultural coffeehouses or the modern chains of coffeeshops. Yet, the chapter is by no means comprehensive but rather will discuss a selection of *mostly* feature films (including several adaptations from Naguib Mahfouz's works discussed in Chapter 4) which are indicative of broader significations. One question we want to unpack here is: what are the new perceptions that cinema offers to deepen our understanding of the café and its role in shaping social relations in the city? Throughout the analysis, our objective is also to address issues about class and gender in relation to the café setting.

The early history of film narrates a crucial story about Egyptian cities and the development of film-making into a large national industry. Nezar AlSayyad states that 'no medium has ever captured the city and the experience of urban modernity better than film';[6] and Tony Fitzmaurice remarks that 'film is *the* urban cultural form *par excellence* … whose origins and destination are tied with the fortunes of the twentieth-century city.'[7] City and cinema became 'lived social realities',[8] and similar to other countries, cinema in Egypt 'had a striking and distinctive ability to capture and express spatial complexity, diversity and social dynamism of the city through *mise-en-scène*, location filming, lighting, cinematography, and editing.'[9] The tempo and spatiality of city life, flow of capital and the human condition in it fascinated Egyptian film-makers as demonstrated by the repertoire of films from the early period. In this way, cinema was not only part and parcel of the process of modernity in the city, but was one that visually illustrated, commented on and critiqued this process. What makes cinema different, as Mark Shiel argues, is its ability to 'illuminate the lived spaces of the city and urban societies', and hence he perceives cinema as 'primarily a spatial system'.[10]

Space, movement and time are inextricably tied into cinematic expression, and the framing of space is used to deconstruct the social reality around us with the purpose of articulating new meanings and significations within specific timeframes. As highlighted in the introductory chapter, it was Henri Lefebvre who pioneered the research on the meaning of social space, specifically in the city. In *The Production of Space*, he makes this observation:

> When we evoke 'energy', we must immediately note that energy has to be deployed within a space. When we evoke 'space', we must immediately indicate what occupies that space and how it does so: the deployment of energy in relation to 'points' and within a timeframe. When we evoke 'time', we must immediately say what it is that moves or changes therein. Space considered in isolation is an empty abstraction; likewise energy and time.[11]

Lefebvre's influential theory about social space and the everyday relations shaping it, as well as his emphasis on the 'body', 'language', and time and energy as essential elements comprising this space have found root in the cinematic field. For example, James Williams states that 'cinema is very specifically, and above all, the concrete, existential experience of space that connects the public, cinematographic cocoon, the worlds projected on to the screen ..., and the individual realms of sensory and mental perception'.[12] Williams quotes the film critic Stephen Heath in his reference to space as 'the superior unity that ties a film to its spectator'.[13] The constant camera movement in different directions and the manipulation of shots and montage are tools which enable the film-maker to capture both objective (physical) and subjective (mental and emotional) spaces. Thus, the 'potential for such interspaces appears limitless', according to Williams.[14] Within this cinematic frame, the sensory experience of sound is integral to our *affective* perception of the film. As Williams observes: 'The result is a fluid set of inner and outer sonic and auditory spaces, making hearing a multidimensional, acoustic space.'[15] In the following parts, these concepts which integrate cinema, urban space, time and energy will be explored in relation to the representation of the café in Egyptian films.

In a TV show entitled *Qahwet Ba'ra: multaqa al combarss* ('Ba'ra Café: The Extras' Meeting Place) produced by al-Nahar channel (2017),[16] the reporter meets with Ahmed al-Zanati, the present owner of Ba'ra Café, a famous *ahwa baladi* which opened in 1932 on Emad Elddin street in downtown Cairo where both star and background actors and actresses used to meet. Ahmed tells about how the café came to be known by this name in reference to its original owner Mohammad al-Zanati (Ahmed's late uncle). It was the well-known actor Rushdi Abaza who gave the uncle the nickname *Ba'ra*, to signify his tall and well-built physique. Ahmed narrates the history of the café and its popularity not only among actors but also among all those who worked in film production: directors, cinematographers, make-up artists, designers, producers and many others. He adds: 'I used to get phone calls all the time from famous people who wanted to talk to these workers or actors. Their meeting point was here.' Ba'ra Café has seen generations of people in the film industry frequenting it, and the café itself figured in some films such as *Garei al-Wuhoush* (Race of the Beasts) made in 1987.[17] According to Ahmed al-Zanati, the café was like their home and its walls are witness to the history of Egyptian film-making in the city. It remains to this day decorated with portraits and pictures of iconic actors. However, the place started to lose its special customers gradually with the rise of mobile phones and social media networks.[18]

This symbiotic relation between the café and cinema in real life, particularly in downtown Cairo and Alexandria, carries an important tradition which we can trace in the present day as well. For example, we always see several cafés opening 24 hours around cinemas (or entertainment venues in general). This is most notable when we consider cinema-houses such as Odeon or Miami, for instance. The front and back streets around these cinemas, located on the busy Cairene Talaat Harb Street, are vibrant with multiple *ahawi*. Another example is Zawya cinema (at the back of the old Odeon) which used to open onto several cafés that became the meeting points for large numbers of young artists and writers. In September 2018, Zawya moved to a new venue on Emad Elddin Street, which is itself busy with many cafés. This demonstrates that the *ahwa baladi* continues to play a significant role in the life of the cinema industry as a social hub where culture is discussed and produced.

The reader will also notice that most of the films discussed here that portray the café and its culture belong to the melodrama genre. We explore the reasons that might have led Egyptian producers to prefer this type of cinematic approach when representing the culture and urban living patterns of the popular classes who inhabit the *ahwa baladi*. Broadly speaking, Egyptian cinema is well-known for the use of melodrama especially in the early period of black-and-white film-making. As film critic Viola Shafik remarks: 'After the introduction of sound, melodrama was frequently combined with the musical film form, engendering some of the most distinguished box office hits of the Egyptian film industry and reaching out eventually into other genres such as realism and action film.'[19] Through introducing narratives of love, sacrifice, betrayal, victimization and patriotism, especially during the colonial era, the melodrama genre enhanced the musical, tragic and comedic elements of the early films and made cinema popular among urban residents. According to Shafik: 'Individual happiness and love stood on one side, while tradition and family rested on the other.'[20] Egyptian films of the 1930s, 1940s and 1950s are famous for their overwhelming melodramatic plots where good usually wins over evil, and the lovers are happily reunited in the end despite the hardships they go through in life.

The *ahwa* as a fundamental element of the urban alley (*hara*)

In black-and-white films of the 1940s and 1950s, the traditional *ahwa baladi* was usually situated in the popular neighbourhoods (*ahiaa sha'biyya*) of the big cities where we meet working-class characters as well as *mo'allimin* (merchants, landlords or shop owners). The *ahwa* was closely linked to the customary way of life of the popular alley (or *hara* in the Egyptian vernacular) with its narrow back streets and 'subaltern' characters. It often reflected men from different social and educational backgrounds and professions sitting side by side, thus crossing class barriers. It was where these male characters found a refuge and social space to enjoy drinks, smoke and exchange news about politics and their neighbourhood. It was also the place where men bonded, fraternized and shared their joys and sorrows. The cinematic lens has depicted how frequenting the café and smoking shisha were signifiers of manliness, hence reinforcing the image of the 'masculine man' and his authority in the patriarchal power structure of Egyptian society. Thus, if we use Henri Lefebvre's broad concept of social space,[21] it can be argued that the café has been the perfect 'concrete place' in filmic depictions where the 'production of everyday social relations' has taken place among Egyptian men.

The traditional alley has been accentuated in Egyptian cinema, to a large extent, as a patriarchal structure where women are either confined to their homes or inhabiting other public spaces, but not the traditional café. For example, in the three film adaptations from Naguib Mahfouz's epic novel *al-Harafish*, published in 1977 and in an English translation by Catherine Cobham under the same title in 1995, namely *al-Tout wal Nabbout* (The Mulberry and the Club, 1986),[22] *al-Gou'* (Hunger, 1986),[23] and *al-Harafish* (1986),[24] the café is the meeting place of the *futuwwa* (i.e. the powerful male chief of the alley) and his men. Cobham has left the title of Mahfouz's novel untranslated but she writes in the 'Translator's Note' that the historical meaning of *harafish* is rabble or riffraff; however, in the novel it means the common people in a 'positive' sense, or 'those who are in menial jobs, casual workers, and the unemployed and the homeless'.[25] The *futuwwa* used to be reflected in literature and cinema as an essential 'unit' of any alley, a man of heroic qualities who stood in the face of hardships and external enemies to defend the people of his community. Through this image, power relations are clearly defined in the urban alley in the sense that each *futuwwa* had his territory which could not be trespassed by others. On the other hand, the *futuwwa* was reworked in cinematic representations to reflect the figure of the oppressor who exploited the poor and vulnerable, and in some films became symbolic of the despotic ruler/dictator. But despite the numerous depictions of the *futuwwa*, the main characteristic remains to be his hyper-masculinity: his deep, loud voice; fearlessness of enemies; well-built physique; his traditional attire of the long gown (*galabiyya*); manly features especially the mustache and muscles; and his pronounced patriarchal authority over the people around him. In this way, cinema has shown the *futuwwa* inhabiting the *ahwa* as a second home.

In juxtaposition to the representation of the *ahwa* as a masculine and patriarchal urban space, some iconic musical comedies portrayed it in a more light-hearted manner. Films starring the two monologists and actors Ismail Yassin and Shukoukou, and others starring singer and actor Abdel Halim Hafez such as *Sharei' al-Hobb* (Love Street, 1958)[26] capture this motif: impoverished protagonists who roam the streets looking for work and come back at the end of the day to the café to rest and meet with friends. In *Love Street*, we see how the main protagonist Mene'im starts his career in music and singing from the small music shop in the alley situated next door to the café, as we follow his trajectory when he emerges later as a star singer but who does not abandon his humble beginnings or his neighbours. Once again we see how the café serves as a second home, if not the first, for those who could not even afford to rent a room on the roof of a building.

In these melodramatic comedies and musicals, the café's function was visualized as a social and entertainment place, an integral part of the alley's everyday life similar to other entities which played a more practical function such as the grocery shop, the barbershop, the butcher, the bakery, and the vegetable and fruit shop. But perhaps the first film in early Egyptian cinema that visually composed the main elements of the alley in a way to reflect a social-realist form was *al-'Azeema* (Determination) made in 1939.[27] The film is a classic of Egyptian cinematic history precisely because the main actions are shot in the alley while portraying the protagonists in a realistic rather than a farcical or satiric manner. The film opens with a panoramic shot to show the physical constituents which we find in any urban alley: the café where men spend their time chatting and bonding; the barbershop; the butcher and the bakery shop. Director Kamal Selim makes the alley relatable to the viewer by situating the two main protagonists Mohammad and Fatima as the son and daughter of the barber and the bakery owner, respectively. They fall in love and we see the happy ending when they are reunited in marriage after they encounter many hardships. As Viola Shafik observes:

> The peculiarity of *Determination* lies in the alley and its inhabitants. This was in sharp contrast to other films at that time. The familiar surroundings of ordinary people were not pictured at all or only briefly and without details, even if those people were represented as main characters. In Selim's film the vivid life of the alley is the main element of the plot. Passers-by, traders, visitors to the café, and inhabitants of the small houses, all take part in the action and show deep interest in what happens to the protagonist and his bride.[28]

In the film, the café takes centre stage as the main place for socialization and entertainment. It is characterized by the presence of its owner or *mo'allim* smoking his special shisha, the waiter or *qahwagi* who moves around to take orders and bring drinks to the tables, and the men themselves sitting in groups playing backgammon, smoking and drinking. Furthermore, in films produced after *Determination*, we see that this specific motif of locating the café in the alley reoccurred to point to how the alley itself with its essential elements was evolving as an urban space in the eyes of directors. For instance, in *al-Souq al-Sowda* (Black Market, 1945),[29] another classic social-realist film, the *ahwa* which has the title 'Café of Workers and Government Employees for its owner Ahmed Wafia Mohsen' plays a different role: it is where the customers gather to listen to the radio and discuss political or business affairs. The film opens with the year 1939 and the news about the eruption of the Second World War where the residents of a *sha'bi* (popular) neighbourhood of Cairo hear this announcement on the radio while congregating inside and outside the café. The war news was of deep concern to the Egyptians (as we have seen in some of Naguib Mahfouz's novels) due to the presence of the British colonial force. The consequences of the war would certainly impact people's lives and would lead to sharp rises in the price of basic commodities such as sugar, flour, rice and tea.

But some merchants, like Abu Mahmoud in the film, found an opportunity during the war to maximize their profits and become wealthy. Together with another fellow merchant in the alley, Abu Mahmoud bought all kinds of goods and stored them to be sold later at higher prices. He and people like him created a 'black market' which had a detrimental impact on the economy and the poorer sectors of the society. The café of their alley is where conversations about the changing economic situation take place and where the emerging wealthy merchants meet to finalize business deals. Gradually, the alley itself changes and the relationships between its residents also transform and grow tense and violent. Everyone can feel the widening social gap between the merchant class who are becoming richer, and the majority who are growing poorer and unable to find the basic goods. In this representation, the alley comes to symbolize the bigger society during the war years. *Black Market* was made in the final year of the war and provided a damning critique of the aggressive capitalist market forces during the war and how this transformed social and class relations.

Indeed, the representation of the traditional café acquires further complexity with the film *Zoqaq al-Madaq* (Midaq Alley),[30] which was released in 1963 and adapted from Naguib Mahfouz's novel under the same title (discussed in Chapter 4). Similar to the novel, the film's narrative shows Kersha's Café as the main vibe of the alley where the men meet and socialize. The café as recreated here turns from a mere social sphere that has a lasting presence in any Egyptian urban alley (as in earlier films) to a metaphor that signifies the passage of time and transition from an old to a new way of life shown through the trajectories of female and male characters. It can be argued that the film has immortalized the traditional *ahwa* by giving it a distinct 'Egyptianness' of sorts. As the characters communicate in the film in vernacular Egyptian-Arabic as opposed to the classical Arabic language in the novel, the narrative itself also transformed significantly to make the characters more grass-roots and relatable. The clothes they adopted and the *mise-en-scène* of the *hara* with its narrow rooms, small shops, dark corners and the close proximity of its characters to one another made the film effective visually among millions of viewers. *Midaq Alley* remains as one of the classics of Egyptian cinema and has never lost its popularity over the decades even for the younger generations.

However, the cinematic lens has focused more prominently on Hamida's character development, the young woman who turns from a humble girl living in Midaq alley to a sex worker who elopes with Farag the pimp, which eventually leads to her demise and murder. Whereas the novel was not meant to be a moral tale, as argued in Chapter 4, it is clear that the film aimed to magnify the social and economic circumstances that drove Hamida to run away from the alley. She is characterized as a victim and the film expands on the sex industry which was prevalent in Egypt during the war years by introducing new female characters who suffered from poverty and found themselves entangled in this exploitative network. At the end of the film, it is Hamida who is killed by a foreign soldier not her fiancé Abbas as we read in the novel. It is a tragic melodramatic conclusion to a story of a girl who lost her way and no one was able to save her.

Modifications of the original literary text when adapting it to cinema were often made to Mahfouz's novels and short stories, the most notable example of which is *The Cairo Trilogy*, where the filmic adaptations came to divert in key elements from the original narratives. It is well known that even though Mahfouz himself wrote many film scripts, he did not rework any scripts out of his own novels. He left this task to other prolific film scriptwriters.[31] In fact,

Mahfouz held a number of posts within the state-run cinema organizations,[32] including his role as director of the Censorship Authority for many years during the Nasser era. Thus, he was fully aware that not all storylines or characters in his own novels could be adapted to cinema. The Egyptian cinema industry was flourishing during the 1950s and 1960s; it had to attract larger audiences and make more profits. It played a powerful role in disseminating the patriotic rhetoric of the new military regime and the pan-Arab ideology. Hence, the melodrama genre was enormously effective in fulfilling these goals, leading to the wide screening of Egyptian films in other Arab countries.

In another popular film, *Baladi wi Khiffa* (Traditional and Sweet) made in 1950,[33] we encounter Umm Za'bal's Café, a traditional *ahwa baladi* which is run by the strong female *mo'allima* (manageress and landlady) Umm Za'bal. The film is a musical comedy, hence there is emphasis on farce and humour. Umm Za'bal and her café are situated within a broader plot about two sweethearts from the same neighbourhood, Mahrous and Hannouma, who are passionate about music and cinema. They are engaged to be married, but their impoverished financial circumstances are a barrier to their matrimony. Each one of them dreams of becoming a star: Mahrous as a famous singer, and Hannouma as a cinema star. The narrative focuses on their trajectories but also locates them within the wider community of their 'Bilhana wil Shifa' alley.

At the start of the film, Umm Za'bal is portrayed as a tough woman, strongly built and smoking shisha in her own café, thus inhabiting a traditionally male social space. She has inherited the café and the house from her deceased husband, and she rents out the flats to her neighbours. She is shown to embody *masculine* qualities in order to survive among other *mo'allimin* (landlords). She is feared in the whole alley because she has the power of money and authority, but also ridiculed by her female neighbours precisely because of her masculine role as the café manageress. Her name is indicative, as Abu Za'bal is one of Egypt's most feared prisons. By introducing this pun on the name Za'bal, the character is represented in a farcical manner, hence reinforcing stereotypes about femininity and masculinity. In this social context, the *ahwa* is a place for women *only* if they exhibit such masculine qualities. It can also be argued that Umm Za'bal is the counter-image of Hamida in *Midaq Alley*; in the way she is rich, rooted in the *hara*, independent and strengthened by her economic status. She is a matriarch whose position as the café owner makes her more exposed to the outside world than other women of the alley. She deals with all types of people which has given her a distinct social role and experience. Thus, through her character, the gender roles are reversed but still denote an unequal relation of power based on material superiority.[34]

Umm Za'bal's café is central in the alley where different characters meet and entertain themselves, but also where they come together in her presence to share their grievances seeking her advice and help. The film depicts how the café is an open space even in a small alley where the customers form a closely-knit social support network. In this way, the contrasting characteristics of the *ahwa* are highlighted: it can be perceived as an 'egalitarian' space (only in some, not all locations) where men from different social classes sit side by side; but it can also be the space where masculine qualities are expressed and inflated. Yet, the film is in essence a celebration of cinema and art, when Umm Za'bal convinces Hannouma and her mother that the former should use her talent to work in cinema. This openness to the production of art was key to Egyptian film narratives as a major theme in the first half of the twentieth century. Once again, it demonstrates the centrality of cinema in expanding the cultural life of the city and how this art comes to be part of people's cultural consumption patterns, even within marginalized and working-class neighbourhoods. As a musical comedy, the film ends on a happy melodramatic note when we see the two main protagonists' dreams of working in the cinema and music industries come true.

In a later film made in 1981, *Qahwet el Mawardi* (Mawardi Café),[35] adapted from a novel by Mohammad Galal, the narrative sheds light on a different era, when president Sadat's open-door economic policy led to transformations in class relations. The Cairene *hara* has drastically changed from what we have seen in the black-and-white films of previous decades. We do not find the same kind of 'unity' or 'coherence' in the *mise-en-scène* of the alley, but rather a close-up on how individuals' lives have grown fragmented and social ties damaged and broken. The film's events take place in the late 1970s where we see Mo'allim Ibrahim el Mawardi, the café owner, as the patriarch and most respected person in the alley. His rival is Mo'allim Abu Sinna who has just come out of prison. Abu Sinna wants to control the alley and appropriate the café so he can turn it into a big shop. It is the era of heightened consumerist capitalism and the importation of foreign commodities which were still novel to the Egyptian market.

Abu Sinna is involved in fraudulent trade deals facilitated by the new laws in the country, but he is much hated and feared in the alley. The narrative focuses on the conflict between these two characters to point to the crossroad the country was in at the time: should people maintain their traditional value system of fraternity and compassion, or should they uproot their way of life for the sake of material greed and profit? These issues are observed by one of the protagonists, Ahmed the journalist, who attempts to write a novel about the neighbourhood but is shot dead later in the film because he became a threat to the newly emerging class of small businessmen. Ahmed's death comes as a wake-up call for the *hara* whose inhabitants were beginning to lose their morals and follow Abu Sinna's commands. The alley here is visualized as a metaphor for the country and the café is the central place where people meet and discuss their concerns with the patriarch Mo'allim el Mawardi. The film concludes with a melodramatic resolution to the conflict where good defeats evil and we see the residents reuniting around Mawardi and his daughter Farawla.

The café as a witness to the deterioration of urban living

Throughout the 1980s and 1990s, we observe how the motif of the fragmentation of the traditional alley was depicted in several popular films where this urban space came to bear witness to the remarkable changes that had constituted a 'malaise' in Egyptian cities: the sharp rise in unemployment, the unprecedented levels of urban poverty, the widespread use of drugs among youths, the inability to find decent housing in the big cities, the deterioration in the standard of public schools and universities, domestic violence against women and children, and much more. Such social ills led to the depiction in cinema of alienated, lonely, stoned or violent characters who had lost their bearing, or even their identity, in huge crowded cities that seemed to lose touch with humanity. These films were pointing to the social manifestations of the neoliberal era and how individuals from the low-income strata were struggling to make a living. The alley with its transformed identity was reflected visually in detail to mirror the breakdown in physical infrastructure caused by dysfunctional state institutions: lack of clean water; constant power cuts; crowded roads filled with garbage; air, food and land pollution; poor housing conditions and narrow dilapidated rooms where people are crammed because they have nowhere else to go.

The new-realist films of this era by directors such as Mohammad Khan, Atef al-Tayyeb, Khayri Bishara, Ossama Fawzi, Magdi Ahmed Ali, Radwan al-Kashif and Daoud Abdel Sayyed focused on how the protagonists had to cling to one another in their small communities to be able to survive, and one place where men were still able to meet and socialize was the *ahwa baladi*. Famous films such as *Youm Morr, Youm Helw* (Sour Day, Good Day, 1988) which starred the legendary actress Faten Hamama;[36] *al-Kitkat* (Kitkat, 1991),[37] a cinematic adaptation of Ibrahim Aslan's novel *The Heron* (discussed in Chapter 3); and *Leih ya Banafseg* (Violet Flowers, Why?, 1993),[38] show the urban alley in this new light, through an illustration of the bottom layer of society to convey to the viewers the forceful changes which big cities, especially Cairo, were experiencing.

In this context, such representations encapsulate once again what scholar Asef Bayat has termed 'the city-inside-out', which we have highlighted in earlier chapters, where the urban poor are constantly present on the streets while taking their activities outdoors. But what cinema has done here is to show in meticulous detail the physical decay and mental deterioration of the characters within neoliberal economies. It is indeed the 'necessity to survive and live a dignified life', as Bayat argues,[39] which drives these impoverished characters in the films to carry out their activities into the public space. In fact, we repeatedly see in some of the new-realist films of the 1980s and 1990s how the café is represented as the place where the 'subaltern' characters 'express their grievances and resolve their problems'.[40] It is true that the characters here attain some autonomy in the public space outside the realm of state institutions and regulations, but they are still tied and restricted by their poverty and the increasingly narrowing margin of accessibility to educational and work opportunities. It is suggested in these films that the traditional *hara* has lost its core of social unity and integration.

The coffeehouse and political dissent

In the Egyptian national imaginary, the coffeehouse has another epistemic dimension in the way it has been linked to different waves of struggle against colonial rule and foreign invasions during the later part of the nineteenth century and throughout the twentieth century. Al Jazeera Documentary channel has produced a series of short films about landmark coffeehouses from across the Arab world including Egypt. In a number of the Egyptian films, the interviewees narrate heroic tales that they have experienced themselves or were conveyed to them by their parents or grandparents about public figures, military heroes, writers and freedom fighters who were involved in the struggle for independence and how the coffeehouse was the place where they hid, held their meetings, printed their leaflets or organized their demonstrations. As discussed in earlier chapters, one such coffeehouse is Café Riche in the heart of downtown Cairo. This coffeehouse opened in 1908 and was owned by foreigners until the year 1960 when the first Egyptian Abdel Malak Mikhail Salib bought it and whose family still owns the café at the time of writing this book.[41] In the documentary entitled 'Old Coffeehouses: Café Riche' (2015),[42] we learn about the history of political dissent which the café was home to during the 1919 revolution, and also about its cultural value in the eyes of novelists and poets.[43]

For example, the well-known novelist Ibrahim Abdel Meguid and late poet Sayyed Higab narrate the literary history of Riche and how the place shaped and influenced their own writing experiences during the 1960s and 1970s through the rich debates they took part in, and how they read and commented on each writer's work in the presence of great figures of the previous generation such as Naguib Mahfouz and Tharwat Abaza. It was 'the destiny' of any serious writer to inhabit Riche during those decades, as Abdel Meguid puts it. Other interviewees in the film tell about the back garden which was an extension of the café and used as a theatre where singers such as Umm Kulthoum in her early career sang as well as the legendary singer Mounira al-Mahdiyya; and where theatre pioneers such as Fatima (Rosa) Alyoussef and her husband Mohammad Abdel Quddous performed.

In addition to Café Riche's cultural value among numerous writers, artists and journalists, we also meet in the film the architect Abbas Mohammad Abbas who led the renovation work of the café years ago after it was damaged during the 1992 earthquake. This was the point when they discovered the basement (cellar) where the revolutionaries hid to print their political leaflets during the 1919 revolution (the story which possibly inspired author Ahmed

Mourad when he wrote his novel *1919* – discussed in Chapter 3). Architect Abbas remarks that the political events during and after the First World War influenced Riche's trajectory. With the breakout of the war, the allied forces who were present in Egypt established their headquarters at Savoy Hotel which was located opposite Riche. At that time, the café opened onto the pavement similar to the Parisian style of *café trottoir*, hence it became the meeting point where journalists and foreign correspondents reported on the war as they received the news first-hand from the headquarters. It was also the period when ordinary Egyptian citizens came to meet the journalists sitting at the café in order to voice their grievances. But Riche continued to play a political role in later decades among the intellectual class of Cairo, as narrated by several interviewees in the film. It was the hub where many statements and petitions were discussed, written and signed, where political movements in art and literature were shaped and formed and where numerous protests were launched, including the time of the 2011 revolution and its aftermath.

This particular example, and others as we saw with older cafés like Matatya, indicate that it was commonplace in real life for coffeehouses to be home for political and revolutionary dissent, hence we find representations of this theme in Egyptian cinema as well. Several writers, including Ibrahim Abdel Meguid, have pointed out that Naguib Mahfouz was inspired by Café Riche when he wrote his novella *Karnak Café* (published in 1974 and discussed in Chapter 4). It was made into a film under the same title in 1975.[44] The film weaves the four parts of the novella into a linear story; whereas the original text voices a clear indictment against the violations of citizens' rights by the Intelligence and Secret Police apparatuses under Nasser, the film does not stop at this representation but expands the story to show support for the Sadat regime in the aftermath of the 6 October 1973 war. The opening of the film diverts completely from the novella, as it begins with an announcement on the radio of the October War victory and the crossing of the Suez Canal by Egyptian soldiers. We see the characters at Karnak Café gathered around Qurunfula the manageress while cheering for this victory. In this first opening scene, we also encounter Ismail al-Sheikh sitting at the café on his own, lost and broken, but once he hears about the victory he immediately rises and leaves the café. The next scene shows Ismail approaching the university hospital where he used to study and work, hoping to volunteer to treat the wounded of the war. He accidentally sees his ex-fiancée Zeinab Diab, who had progressed in her life after she overcame the trauma of rape and torture which she was subjected to in prison. She graduated from the Medical School and became a doctor. When Ismail is refused entry to the hospital, Zeinab convinces the director to permit him to join in. After the opening credits, the viewer begins to follow the story from the start through flashbacks. The film focuses on the trajectory of the three university students Hilmi, Zeinab and Ismail and their meetings at Karnak Café where their political views were formed and voiced.

The café here is represented as a political and cultural urban space, home to the intellectual class (similar to Café Riche) where the manageress herself is open to a wide range of views expressed freely within the walls of her café. Indeed, the viewer feels that al-Karnak is an ideal place which embraces people from all walks of life. The students who study arts and sciences gather every week to discuss literature and politics with esteemed writers. They exchange their views without constraints. However, they are unaware of the presence of *mukhbireen* (spies or informers) who eventually report on the students and lead to their arrest and torture in the military prison. Even Qurunfula is unaware of them until Hilmi, her lover, is killed in prison as a result of the informers' reports. The film also magnifies the sharp transformation which Zeinab goes through after her rape, when she agrees to visit the café to report on political dissent to Khaled Safwan, her torturer in the prison.

But while the novella concludes with open-ended uncertainty about the future of the country and the protagonists, the film closes on the 'new hope' which the October War victory has brought to the country. We see a clear support for the 15 May 1971 'Corrective Revolution' or *thawrat al-tasshih*, a term coined by the Sadat regime to signify a new approach for 'correcting' the wrongdoing of the previous regime. We see in the film that Ismail, together with the other political detainees, are pardoned and released from prison as a result of the May corrective revolution's new measures, whereas in the novella they are released after the 1967 war defeat. In this way, by portraying the 1973 war victory as symbolic of a new era and a new hope, we observe how the content of one of Mahfouz's works was modified to strike melodramatic notes about patriotism and nationalism, so as to fit within the political climate of the time and show support for the new president.

Forging friendships in the vast social spatiality of the *ahwa*

One of the most significant aspects of the *ahwa baladi* as represented in a huge output of Egyptian cinema remains to be its role in consolidating friendships and brotherly support specifically among men. A recurring motif shows the café as the reference point where the characters can be found if they are needed for work or any other business. In other words, it is customary knowledge that 'the man of the house' will be found at the neighbourhood's café. In a number of films adapted from Naguib Mahfouz's novels, for example *Khan al-Khalili* (1967),[45] *Qasr al-Shouq* (Palace of Desire, 1967),[46] and *al-Sukarriyya* (Sugar Street, 1973),[47] we watch scenes of middle-class male characters meeting at the *ahwa* to chat or smoke shisha. In these adaptations, the café as a masculine social space par excellence is reinforced over and again through the visual medium.

However, what is unique about cinematic representations lies in the manipulation of 'social spatiality' and the proximity or distance between characters. In the café, although the physical space is usually limited, and in many cases crowded, the film-maker can utilize the emotions and conversations expressed by the characters to convey a vast range of sociability between them. It is an affective experience which the viewer is also party to. For instance, the viewer can 'feel' whether the characters sitting side by side in the narrow space of the café are joyful to be together or constrained or apprehensive and so on. Through their interaction, bodily gestures and facial expressions, which are manipulated by various shots, the film-maker is able to define the emotional chart between them. This is significant because the camera lens transforms visually the limited *physical* space of the café which we are used to frequent in real life into an enormous *affective* space where social relations are explored and critiqued.

One key film which denotes this concept effectively is *al-Saqqa Mat* (The Water Carrier Is Dead, 1977),[48] an iconic work directed by Salah Abu Seif and adapted from a story by writer Youssef al-Siba'i. The film was co-produced by the Misr International Film Company, which was established by another legendary film-maker (Youssef Chahine), and the Tunisian Company for Cinematic Development and Production. The events take place in Islamic

Cairo, specifically in al-Azhar area in the year 1921, when clean water for drinking and cooking was scarce and used to be distributed to households by the water carrier. It is an allegorical story meant to be timeless, and a quiet philosophical contemplation of life, death, love and friendship. The acclaimed Egyptian film critic Sami al-Salamouni referred to it 'not only as the best film by Salah Abu Seif so far but also the best in the last ten years [between 1967 to 1977]'.[49] Moreover, writer Hashim al-Nahhas who includes a conversation in his book about the film with Abu Seif himself, observes that the work was 'a poetic journey about life and death' marking a highly sophisticated cinematic approach in the film-maker's trajectory.[50]

In the film, we follow how the two main protagonists Shousha (the water carrier) and Shehata (a funeral assistant) develop a remarkable friendship through their meetings at the café while drinking tea, smoking shisha and chatting about their lives. Each influences the other in a different way: Shousha enlightens Shehata's soul through his ethics and commitment to work and family; and Shehata revives in Shousha's heart passion and sentimentality after he had buried his emotions with the untimely death of his beloved wife. At first, Shehata convinces his new friend Shousha to accompany him to al-Afandiyya Café in their neighbourhood to hang out, play backgammon and entertain themselves.[51] But gradually their friendship develops through intimate and soul-lifting conversations at the café. They are working-class men who spend the day making a living, but in the evening they frequent the café, the only place where they can afford to socialize. Shousha and Shehata begin to confide in one another their innermost feelings about life, death, passion and desire. The multiple medium shots through which the director frames the two characters, especially while sitting at the café, emphasize the close proximity between them and the growing depth of their friendship.

Shehata, the vagabond who never cares about responsibilities and has no permanent job or shelter, is embraced by Shousha who welcomes him to stay in the spare room of his humble flat. In one scene of the film while the two protagonists are conversing at the café, Shehata says: 'Life for me is like a free business endeavor, sometimes the business goes well and at other times it doesn't. I'm neither afraid of life nor believe that it will stay forever. God damn this life, it can go anytime it wants.' But Shousha shows his friend another way of living by being compassionate towards others, so as to be valued and respected.

And Shehata in turn convinces Shousha that he has to 'snatch his right to life' and to reignite his passions and desires, since 'death will come to us anyway'.

Yet, the café here is also where pimps and drug dealers sit side by side with the other customers. Shehata strikes a deal with a pimp so he can spend a night with Aziza whom he has fallen in love with. But her price is very expensive for Shehata, so he can only *dream* of being with her while working hard to save the money for that promised night when they will be together physically. Ironically, it is Shehata, the true lover of life, who dies suddenly as a result of a drug overdose before fulfilling his dream of making love with Aziza. He leaves behind his friend Shousha completely broken and on the verge of losing faith in God. One of the most powerful sequences in the film is when we watch Shousha alone in the cemetery voicing an internal monologue about the evilness of death. *The Water Carrier* underscores a sophisticated perspective of gender relations and the construction of manhood at that time in the early-twentieth-century city. Similar to the other films discussed above, the café is portrayed as central to the neighbourhood's urban living, where friendships grow and change lives.

Another film made three decades after *The Water Carrier*, entitled *Malik wi Ketaba* (Heads & Tails, 2006),[52] introduces the viewer to a more contemporary friendship between a middle-aged college professor, Dr Mahmoud, and a young woman, Hind, who is an aspiring actress. At the start of the film, Dr Mahmoud is portrayed as a strict, arrogant professor at the High Institute of Drama, who is feared and disliked by his students. His style of dress and bombastic manner of talking and walking indicate that he is in full control of his life. He is settled in his marriage and in love with his wife, but his life is showing signs of monotony and dullness. Suddenly, his seemingly stable life is turned upside down and his image of himself is shattered to pieces when he discovers that his wife has a lover. The shock of this discovery causes him a severe psychological disequilibrium. He feels that everything he believed in was a lie. He divorces his wife, and as he takes time off work he starts frequenting the café. Interestingly, the café scenes are set at al-Horriyya coffeehouse, a historic and well-known place in downtown Cairo. This coffeehouse is characterized by its large space and multiple mirrors. People from all walks of life sit there, both women and men who belong to different social and age groups, to socialize and enjoy soft and alcoholic drinks.[53]

At this coffeehouse, Dr Mahmoud starts a new life. He begins to make new acquaintances and finds himself involved in trivial chats. His friends ask him about his job and whether he has met famous actors. Mahmoud finds in their company a different type of sociability, away from his enclosed world of books, academia, students and exams. His voiceover tells us that among these people he can create the image he likes of 'Dr Mahmoud' and he can talk about anything. This affective experience in particular takes us back to the idea of how the 'stranger', ironically, finds himself at home in the café environment. And so we see how frequenting the coffeehouse comes to be a habit of Mahmoud. One day while he is playing chess there, a beautiful young woman, Hind, comes and greets him. She knew him because she often visits the High Institute of Drama to meet her friends, and she has heard about him. Even though Mahmoud behaves arrogantly towards her and in fact ridicules her when she attempts to criticize his teaching style, their relationship later develops into a deep friendship.

In this film, we do not observe the setting only at al-Horriyya coffeehouse, but we also get a glimpse into the modern café chains where Hind and her friends meet. The viewer can immediately notice the contrast between Mahmoud's generation who spend time at the old coffeehouse in downtown Cairo, and Hind's generation who are more attracted to the Westernized type of coffeeshops like Beano's and Cilantro located in middle-class suburbs. Women feel more at ease in these coffeeshops, and they are not under the male's gaze as in the *ahwa baladi*. In one of the crucial scenes of the film, Dr Mahmoud enters the coffeeshop where Hind and her friends are drinking coffee and chatting, in order to apologize to her for mocking her views in front of the other students. It was now his turn to introduce his real self to her: the warm, generous, sentimental Mahmoud. Director Kamla Abu Zikri here situates the two protagonists first at the coffeehouses as they try to break the ice in their relationship, before they move to the more intimate spaces of the home when their friendship grows deeper over time. Later in the film, Mahmoud confesses through his voiceover that he has fallen in love with Hind, but he will not allow himself to go any further because she is much younger than him and is in love with another man of her age. In their encounters, the viewer can sense a different type of social and gender dynamic where the characters, men and women, young and old, insist on equality and respect as driving forces of their friendship. Mahmoud also admits in the last scene of the film that these young people, his students, have taught him many new things and brought much light and energy to his lonely life.

Conclusion

This chapter has critically addressed a diverse range of films which have represented the café culture in Egyptian cities during different periods since the early stages of the cinema industry in the twentieth century. Our research has shown that there is indeed a symbiotic relation between cinema, city and the *ahwa baladi* where the latter is visualized in films as an integral part of urban space, especially the traditional alley. The café is also imagined in film as a masculine space where men's presence is visible and women are not allowed into this world. However, films made in later periods of the twentieth century show depictions of modern coffeehouses and coffeeshops where female characters are present as a taken-for-granted matter. Times have evolved in the city and women are now more visible in the public domain, even in those places which traditionally were male-oriented. Cinema has also accentuated how coffeehouses have always played a role in forging friendships and a special type of close sociability, in addition to being places for revolutionary work and cultural and political mobilization. In the next chapter, we will follow the trajectory of the café in the world of music and entertainment in Egyptian cities and explore the great degree of its influence on singers and performers.

6

Egyptian singers and performers: An integral relation to the coffeehouse

Introduction: The coffeehouse as an art space for popular singers and performers

As mentioned in Chapter 2, historically, the early Egyptian coffeeshops served as open spaces for art and performance for many singers and various music and dance troupes in the big cities, particularly Cairo. In a way, the coffeeshop helped in the production, dissemination and consumption of popular art, thus making it accessible and relatable to people's everyday lives. This form of art at the café was produced for the people by grass-roots artists, hence shaping the city life in terms of its entertainment activities, and reinforcing a social and cultural bond between urban residents and their favourite artists and coffeehouses.

In Chapter 2, we discussed how the writer and historian Abdel Mon'eim Shemeis has demonstrated that since the late eighteenth century, the Cairo coffeehouses were places for literary and artistic performances, folk music and dance, as well as epic storytelling in different suburbs around the city such as al-Azbakiyya, Boulaq, Emad Elddin, Bab al-Louq and Roud al-Farag, in addition to the ones in al-Azhar area. The coffeehouses continued to play a role as central entertainment places until the first decades of the twentieth century, before the advancement of theatre and cinema.[1]

Shemeis goes on to say that the well-known Egyptian historian Abdel Rahman al-Jabarti had stories to tell about the Cairo coffeehouses in his accounts about the life of Egyptians in the eighteenth and early part of the nineteenth centuries, especially about the coffeehouses located by the Nile in Boulaq. From al-Jabarti's accounts, we learn that the Boulaq coffeehouses used to serve as entertainment venues where performers sang and danced, and others told their folk and heroic tales while playing their traditional *rabab* (ancient lyre instrument).[2] Al Jabarti also mentioned that Boulaq was inhabited by the wealthy sectors of the city, and the whole suburb was famous for hosting writers, poets, musicians, singers and many other artists.[3] In other accounts by scholars and historians, according to Shemeis, the Cairene coffeehouses hosted singers and performers from all walks of life where al-Azbakiyya suburb was well known as a cultural and artistic hub in the city. For example, entertainers included vernacular writers who would perform jokes and satirical anecdotes they had written as social and political critique, while creating a musical rhythm on small drums they carried with them to accentuate the lyrics and attract their audiences' attention.

Some vernacular poets, most famously Bayram al-Tounsi, would perform their improvised poetry following the basic rhythm of the *arghul* instrument (a double-pipe single reed woodwind instrument) which developed into what came to be known as 'arghul Bayram al-Tounsi'.[4] It was also referred to as 'mawwal', a folk type of compiling vernacular lyrics around a particular theme usually punctuating it by using the words: first, second, third and repeating them to end up by composing a full story. Following in the footsteps of al-Tounsi's arghul, the *mawwal* became a popular form of entertainment and political critique in coffeehouses and social gatherings in Cairo in the early decades of the twentieth century.[5]

Furthermore, Shemeis draws attention to how coffeehouses were also central places for the celebration of the religious *mawalid* (festivals in commemoration of Prophet Mohammad's birthday and other revered Muslim saints), as well as for shadow play artists to entertain the customers. He mentions that French scholars who accompanied Bonaparte's military campaign on Egypt (1798–1801) documented in their multivolume book *The Description of Egypt* that the Egyptian coffeehouses witnessed various artistic productions including the performance of songs, dance by professional female artists, vernacular poems and folktales accompanied by the *rabab* instrument, and religious songs and chants.[6] Shemeis further observes that al-Azbakiyya suburb continued into the twentieth century to be the main spot for the artistic and cultural performances at coffeehouses, before stretching to Emad Elddin Street in the downtown of Cairo. Moreover, Roud al-Farag suburb was famous for its coffeehouses by the Nile during the summer when customers attended artistic performances there.[7]

Shemeis crucially mentions that during the French campaign in Egypt and then in the early part of Mohammad Ali's reign, female entertainers in coffeehouses performed erotic and striptease dances, and this was commonplace until Mohammad Ali issued a ban on this type of dance in public places. Shemeis observes that the ban was considered the first to be declared as a form of censorship against artists in Egypt's modern history.[8] He further comments that in his youth in the 1940s and 1950s, he knew of some coffeehouses on Mohammad Ali Street in Cairo (where many artists, musicians and dancers reside and perform) where female dancers were still performing there, and some of those performances were unconventional and erotic.

In contrast to these coffeehouses in places like al-Azbakiyya and Boulaq, al-Azhar area (in Islamic Cairo) was famous for its multiple coffeehouses which were visited by both men of letters and those of religion. Shemeis mentions that writers and artists used to meet and entertain themselves in those coffeehouses until the early morning hours; and one such famous coffeehouse was al-Afandiyya where writers shared their literary output and poetry.[9] In the previous chapter, we pointed to this coffeehouse which figured in the film *The Water Carrier*, but its function in the film is re-created in a different way from the real coffeehouse that existed in al-Azhar. Also, the coffeehouses in al-Hussein area were famous among educated men who met there to discuss literary issues, especially in al-Fishawi coffeehouse. Shemeis himself frequented al-Fishawi when it was a place for iconic writers and poets to meet in the 1940s and 1950s (including Naguib Mahfouz). Shemeis remarks that al-Fishawi's renown was drawn from the great value of men of letters who visited it.[10] He also mentions Sha'ban café which used to be located in the small square opposite al-Hussein mosque, and where religious singers (most famously Mohammad al-Kahlawi and Sheikh Ali Mahmoud) used to frequent it especially during the month of Ramadan, to sing chants in praise of the Prophet and recite religious verses from the Quran in rhythmic melodies in the presence of a large audience.[11] Furthermore, calligraphers, editors and technicians who worked in the print and publishing industries often sat at al-Hussein coffeehouses because the area itself was filled with print houses and bookshops.[12]

Such a vibrant cultural ambience which characterized Cairo's coffeehouses for more than two centuries adds another layer to our understanding of the café space in shaping the urban life of Egyptians. In fact, we can even say that music and dance of different types have contributed to the 'marketing' of coffeehouses as cultural/entertainment places.[13] As Steve Oakes and Gary Warnaby argue: 'The very diversity/cosmopolitanism of music production in a city may be an important factor in its cumulative attraction.'[14] This was certainly the case in the Cairene and Alexandrian coffeehouses which further enriched their cosmopolitan quality. The coffeehouse allowed for the open interaction between the artist, audience (or consumers of the art) and art itself, hence influencing the aesthetic experience by 'demystifying' the concept of 'high art' and leading to the 'co-creation of meaning' between artist and audience.[15] In this context, the traditional Egyptian *ahwa baladi* was a place for popular art to be performed, circulated and consumed.

This lasting vibrancy is captured in a short documentary shot at Zahrat al-Bustan coffeehouse by Al Jazeera Documentary Channel in 2015.[16] As mentioned in Chapter 3, this coffeehouse is one of the most popular in downtown Cairo. A number of writers and artists are interviewed in the film, most notably Salwa Bakr and the late Mikkawi Sa'id (novelists), Magdi Ahmed Ali (film-maker) and Assem Sharaf (painter). These public figures tell about their memories of the place and how they have been frequenting it for decades due to its open and lively atmosphere. Its current owner mentions that the coffeehouse has been an integral part of downtown cultural life for over seventy years. Throughout the film, we see two young men sitting together at the café, one is playing the lute and his friend is drumming the melodies of iconic Arabic songs, thus composing the music track of this short film.

Moreover, in Alexandria, we learn from a short documentary (also made by Al Jazeera Documentary Channel) about Sayyed Darwish café located in the working-class area of Kom el Dikka (where the legendary singer was born and brought up).[17] Darwish used to compose some of his songs at that very café shown in the documentary. His grandson, the famous singer Iman al-Bahr Darwish, also went to the same café and performed his grandfather's songs there. In the documentary, we see the young singer Hazim Shahin, a member of Eskenderella band, singing Sayyed Darwish's songs at the same café in 2015 when the film was made.[18] What this film demonstrates is the close lineage and continuity between past and present generations of singers who have established a relationship with a particular place where their audiences gathered to listen and sing along with them – in this case it is the Sayyed Darwish café that opens onto the street similar to most traditional cafés in Egyptian cities. Once again, we see how popular singers bridged the gap of categorization of 'high' versus 'low' art by gathering with their audience in the café space and on the streets.

These powerful cultural and corporeal elements drawn between the traditional café space and popular music and performance in Egyptian cities does indeed intersect with what is referred to by a number of music scholars and researchers in the West and Australia as a 'music scene'. As Christopher Driver and Andy Bennett argue in their article 'Music Scenes, Space and the Body' (2015), 'the concept of scene has long been associated with urban settings.'[19] Academic research has analysed, for instance, the Chicago blues scene and the London pub rock scene, and many others where 'the notion of music scene becomes a form of collective association and a means through which individuals with different relationships to a specific genre of music produced in a particular space articulate a sense of collective identity and belonging.'[20] In this specific way, the music scene references not only the musicians, performers and producers of the cultural form, but also the audience who become part and parcel of this scene because they contribute to its development and continuation. One can argue that the Egyptian coffeehouse had historically constituted a space for a music scene to take shape, and as a result a collective social sense of belonging to this urban entity took root.

In an article published in 1991 by the Canadian academic Will Straw, he proposes the following in defining the musical scene:

A musical scene … is that cultural space in which a range of musical practices coexist, interacting with each other within a variety of processes of differentiation, and according to widely varying trajectories of change and cross-fertilization. The sense of purpose articulated within a musical community normally depends on an affective link between two terms: contemporary musical practices, on the one hand, and the musical heritage which is seen to render this contemporary activity appropriate to a given context, on the other. Within a musical scene, that same sense of purpose is articulated within those forms of communication through which the building of musical alliances and the drawing of musical boundaries take place. The manner in which musical practices within a scene tie themselves to processes of historical change occurring within a larger international musical culture will also be a significant basis of the way in which such forms are positioned within that scene at the local level.[21]

Although Straw was specifically analysing the changing rock music scene, his apt analysis complicates our perception of the traditional Egyptian coffeehouse because it sheds light on how music has played a fundamental role in foregrounding means of communication, a sense of purpose, alliances and ties between the performers, their audience, the café owners and the workers at these coffeehouses. Here, we encounter a social space that has created a dynamic collective community, where the musical practices themselves have helped concretize these social relations and enhanced them in a specifically metropolitan setting.

It is also relevant here to bring in the voice of one of our interviewees, Khalil, a musician, in his early 50s and plays the traditional Arabic lute instrument. He spoke about his experience in organizing musical and cultural activities at two cafés in Dhaher, a residential area of middle- and working-class communities in Cairo. Khalil relays here this noteworthy experience:

> In 2005, we decided to start a cultural programme at the Jesuit school, where I've been working for many years. I always like to reach out to as many people as possible. So the first activity we started was to invite Hasaballah troupe and walk the streets around the area here [Dhaher] with them playing their music and sing along with them. Of course people on the streets were surprised to see this …. Then, we thought of bringing the activities from the streets to the *ahwa*, and we chose a *hayy sha'bi* [popular suburb] to do this in the Dhaher area: Bab el Bahr. The Bab el Bahr community is mostly composed of manual workers and craftsmen. We went to a café called Gamal, and I spoke with Gamal the owner about our cultural programme. He agreed under the condition that we pay for all our drinks. We chose it because it was a spacious café so we could accommodate many people there.
>
> At Gamal's café, we showed short films, and Hasan el Gereitly's music group also performed there a few times. We also invited el Gereitly's theatre group

to perform a couple of times. This cultural programme continued until 2011, then we moved to another café called Layalina, which is also in Dhaher. Its owner welcomed us and allowed for our performances to take place, but he asked for money. We paid him some money but not much. We used to have a huge audience at these cafés when we held our activities. Lots and lots of people from various age groups came along.

The whole experiment during those 'golden' years was quite unique actually. But then we started to draw the attention of both the Islamists and the police, especially after the 2011 revolution, because of the political content of our activities. So in the end we decided to stop the programme. It was getting dangerous. What is so special about this experiment was the way that we were able to bring together a genuine mix between the local residents and the musicians and actors. We created much space for these different groups to interact and perform together, so the craftsmen for example would perform with the famous musicians such as Fathy Salama. It was a real mix of people, and the *ahwa* as an open space helped us to do this. Everything was acceptable.[22]

Khalil's testimony certainly describes the production of a 'music scene' in a popular area of Cairo, which was possible precisely because it was staged at the *ahwa baladi* and also moving beyond it onto the streets. Once again, we see how this 'concrete place' continues to shape social and cultural relations in Egyptian cities to the present day. In the following parts, we discuss how several Egyptian singers in different time periods were able to forge a strong relation to the theme of coffee and coffeehouse.

The theme of coffee and coffeehouse in popular Egyptian songs

In the early decades of the twentieth century with the emergence of cinema as a new entertainment industry in the country, in particular the musical melodrama genre which became enormously popular, a number of Egyptian singers produced songs which revolved around the theme of 'coffee' and 'coffeehouse'. One iconic work in this repertoire is Asmahan's song 'Ana Ahwa' (I am in Love), which was composed by her brother the great musician Farid al-Atrash and sung in the film *Gharam wa Intiqam* (Passion and Vengeance,

1944).[23] This song is an integral part of the modern archive of songs about the tradition of drinking coffee and sharing it with guests in Egyptian society as an act of hospitality. Asmahan's song is particularly interesting because the singer uses the word *ahwa* in Arabic to refer to two things simultaneously: passion and longing which are indicated by the verb 'ahwa' (I am in love), and the Egyptian colloquial pronunciation of *qahwa* (coffee) as *ahwa*. In the song, Asmahan appears in traditional peasant dress handing cups of coffee to the upper-class guests who are being entertained during a costume party, and sings: '*Ahwa* (coffee), *ana ahwa* (I am in love)', thus bringing together her own passion for the beloved with the passion for coffee. She continues to sing: 'I will serve coffee with my own hands to whoever says I am in love.' Moreover, it is intimated in the lyrics that those in love are unable to sleep at night because they are constantly thinking of the beloved, hence the coffee drink is their sole companion. Such a light-hearted love song performed by one of the most revered music legends at the time made the theme of 'coffee' hugely popular for Egyptian viewers.

But while Asmahan's song is performed in a grand house where the upper-class characters are assembled on a festive occasion, Omar al-Gizawi's witty song 'Itfaddal Gahwa' (Please come in and have some coffee) and his performance of it in the film *Khad el Gamil* (The Sweetheart's Cheeks, 1951) shows a striking contrast in both form and content. The song was composed by the famous singer Abdel Aziz Mahmoud who also plays the main role in the film, and the song takes the form of a humorous sketch. Here, al-Gizawi is singing in the Upper-Egyptian dialect and is dressed in peasant attire, while performing the song as a traditional (*sha'bi*) singer.[24] The song became very popular because of the humour embedded in it, and the way it points to the essential gesture of inviting a passer-by for coffee as an initial introduction to get to know one another and open a conversation. In other words, as an act of hospitality and socialization, Egyptians are used to say this phrase to any guest: 'Please come in and have some coffee (or tea)' even if the guest is busy and has to rush on his or her way.

Moreover, the Nubian singer and composer Ahmed Munib's popular song 'Talab al-ahwa wi ma shribhash' (He asked for coffee and didn't drink it) introduces the listener to an interesting concept about how the way one prefers to drink their coffee at the café could be indicative of this person's mood. For example, Munib sings that his friend (who is implied to be either a male or a female) sat at the café in a 'grumpy state' and asked to drink coffee without sugar; and that his friend asked for coffee and then left without drinking it. The song describes an encounter between the singer and his friend who was supposed to meet him at the café, and when he/she finally appeared, the coffee was ordered but was not drunk.[25]

Hakawi al-Qahawi (Tales from the Coffeehouses): Revival of the coffeehouse theme on Egyptian state TV

During the fasting month of Ramadan of the year 1990, a new state-sponsored programme entitled *Hakawi al-Qahawi* or 'Tales from the Coffeehouses' was first shown on Channel Two to a huge Egyptian audience. The programme included all the successful elements: a popular TV presenter, Samia El Etriby, who interviewed the guests; a specialist on Egyptian popular culture, Yehia Tadrus, who wrote the script for all the episodes; and an engaging opening sequence whose music was composed by the famous musician Yehia Khalil. The programme became a hit and acquired enormous popularity throughout its duration in the 1990s while being a fixture on television during the month of Ramadan. El Etriby, the programme's presenter, would visit various traditional cafés across the country, walk in the narrow passageways in poor, neglected areas and meet ordinary Egyptians going about their daily lives but who were also making their own unique contributions to their small communities through their work, art and cultural performances. El Etriby gave voice to those marginalized communities, listened to their tales, joys, sorrows and dreams, and showed the daily 'heroism' of their struggles to make a living. Gradually, the programme turned into a cultural documentation of many hidden talents in remote villages and small neighbourhoods across Egypt; but interestingly, the main motif throughout its duration was the focus on the traditional café as a meeting place that opens onto the wider streets where El Etriby would conduct her interviews and walk with the interviewees to their residential areas or workplaces. Indeed, the programme touched the hearts of millions of Egyptians because many were able to relate to the interviewees and their survival mechanisms.[26]

Before the start of each episode, El Etriby would recite these vernacular lyrics (in Arabic) which stamped the programme with a *sha'bi* (popular) identity:

The coffeehouse is a whole vibrant world by itself

Where those who are assembling sit next to those who are dreaming

It's a world filled with entertainment but also with wisdom

In it, you find all sorts of people.

Through these simple words, the introduction pointed directly to how the coffeehouse is a significant popular feature of Egypt's social and cultural life where all sorts of stories are told, and where we can meet all types of people. More importantly, the programme succeeded in introducing new talents in various spheres (art, handicrafts, music, performance, etc.), and also interviewing popular artists who had a huge audience but were not visible on state television, such as the Sufi singer Sheikh Yassin al-Tuhami and the Upper Egyptian *rabab* folk musician Rayyes Mitqal.[27] In one of the famous episodes, El Etriby meets with a *qahwagi* (tea/coffee maker) who has installed a small café space under an old tree in front of the Qanatir prison in al-Qanatir al-Khayriyya area, and has been making tea for decades to those who come to visit their relatives inside the prison. After meeting with him, El Etriby walks into the prison and talks to several inmates so as to shed light on their life and dreams after they have completed their sentences.[28] Another popular episode was conducted in a small café, one of the oldest on Mohammad Ali Street, where El Etriby hosted the famous Hasaballah music troupe, the members of whom also reside on this well-known street.[29]

'Tales from the Coffeehouses' revived the popular theme of the traditional café in the minds of Egyptian viewers and investigated their heritage in depth in the past and present. Currently, after almost two decades since the programme had stopped, Egyptian viewers are still able to watch many of its past episodes through the recently launched channel on Egyptian state television, 'Maspero in the Past'.

The coffeehouse as a political site for resistance music in the experience of the Canal Zone cities

In other parts of Egypt, specifically in the Canal Zone cities of Port Sa'id, Isma'iliyya and Suez, the coffeehouse transformed into a 'political site' where singers from different backgrounds gathered to compose patriotic lyrics and songs along with the tunes of their traditional instrument, *simsimiyya*, about resistance against the British colonialists and other invaders of their cities. Simsimiyya is a small, five-stringed lyre that gained popularity in Port Sa'id in the 1930s, where café owners were the first to employ the musicians to entertain the workers and fishermen. This specific association between the simsimiyya songs and the centrality of the coffeehouse within the Canal Zone area as sites of resistance has been documented by popular culture scholars (e.g. D. Reynolds)[30] as one of the most significant musical and political experiences in twentieth-century Egypt.[31]

In one of the short films made by Al Jazeera Documentary Channel entitled *Borset al-Fallah Café* (2015),[32] located in Port Sa'id city on the main Mohammad Ali Street and founded in 1948, its present owner Ali Abdel Meguid Othman tells about both the cultural and political history of the café. Interestingly, the music track which accompanies the interviews in this episode is that of simsimiyya, and we see the two band members, one is a simsimiyya player and the singer who is also drumming to accentuate the tunes, sat at the café performing one of the iconic songs of resistance, 'Port Sa'id the Patriotic City'.

According to Othman, in past decades, this café was the main place that actors, artists, journalists, writers, teachers, judges and lawyers frequented. He remarks that these different groups of people transformed his coffeehouse into a 'microcosm of a nation'. Moreover, it became the centre for the popular resistance movement against the tripartite aggression during the Suez War in 1956. Othman points to bullet holes visible on the café doors which were left as a witness to the aggressive war on the city at the time. His café became the headquarters of the resistance and he tells about the heroic stories of young and old freedom fighters who fought with their lives for the city. Also, during the June War in 1967 and its aftermath, the café continued to play a political role where the underground resistance organized and mobilized for the war effort, as Othman recounts.

In her documentary entitled *Saba' Layali wi Subhiyya* (Seven Nights and a Dawn, 1998),[33] the Lebanese-Egyptian film-maker Arab Lotfi travels to Port Sa'id to document the musical tradition of a group of musicians and singers who have been working together since the early 1980s to revive the heritage of their popular instruments, the simsimiyya and tanbura. By focusing on the simsimiyya music in her film, Lotfi reads the city's history through the medium of its popular music. Her camera captures the musicians, working-class men who have morning jobs, sitting in the evening at al-Labban café in the heart of the city, chatting and composing their lyrics and music. She meets them at the café and documents their public performances on the street in front of their favourite café. She meets other interviewees as well who speak about their political activities during the 1956 Suez War. We also listen to the historian Morsi Sultan, originally from Port Sa'id, talking about how the simsimiyya and damma music (the latter based on Sufi chants and lyrics) characterized the Arab population of his city who lived to the west of the main Mohammad Ali Street, and distinguished them from Western music which was prevalent among the foreigners who lived to the east of the main street. Thus, from its inception in Port Sa'id, the simsimiyya was associated with the Egyptian and migrant working-class communities. In the first part of the twentieth century, the simsimiyya drew large audiences and a new folk music was created. The music and lyrics came to play a role in the national independence movement against colonialism through resistance songs. Later on, during the Suez War, the simsimiyya continued to be a 'voice of resistance' by documenting a history of national struggle through protest songs.

Lotfi explains that the title of her documentary *Seven Nights and a Dawn* also comes from a patriotic song sung by Port Sa'idi popular singers about how their city became a symbol of resistance during the 1956 Suez War. The city and its people fought the tripartite aggression by Britain, France and Israel for seven nights, and on the morning of the eighth day, the coalition forces withdrew. Lotfi remarks: 'It is as if Port Sa'id was remade and recreated through this resistance struggle in seven days.'[34] The popular musical gatherings at cafés where the simsimiyya music is played until the present day are set in such a way as to break down the barriers of gender, class and age. Everyone attending is expected to join in and take part in singing and dancing with the musicians, hence creating an inclusive 'music scene'. Interestingly, it is this same group of musicians in Lotfi's film who later co-founded El Mastaba Centre for Egyptian Folk Music in Cairo. In so doing, their music has been travelling across different Egyptian cities and provinces.

The coffeehouse in song after the January 2011 revolution

Furthermore, our research findings have indicated that the theme of the traditional *ahwa* was revived by a number of younger singers in the aftermath of the 2011 revolution, such as Islam Ali's song 'Qahwa Baladi' and Haidy's song 'Ahwa Baladi', which is also a play on the Arabic verb 'ahwa', and can mean 'traditional café' as well as 'I love Baladi' (my nation). The well-known singer Hamza Namira also performed a song entitled '3alahwa' (At the café) for the radio channel Nogoum FM (FM Stars). We argue that these singers have drawn on the *ahwa* theme because it is one of the most grass-roots features of Egyptian urban life that can be easily associated with the 2011 popular revolution. In 2011, Egyptians from various age, class and gender groups took part in the mass protests and occupied the squares and streets in cities across Egypt. The café theme reflects this diversity, specifically because the traditional café opens its doors onto the streets. Any passers-by (particularly men) can choose to sit at a café on the streets. In our introductory chapter, we explained how the activists and revolutionaries on Tahrir Square and all the area surrounding it created a new spatial map of downtown Cairo and how the outdoor *ahawi* were part of this new urban scene as meeting places for the protestors. Their visibility on the streets with their vast diversity continued in the aftermath of the revolution for at least three years until the authorities started to close down some of these cafés.[35]

In Haidy's music clip 'Ahwa Baladi',[36] the young singer draws the main thematic element of the song from the traditional café and its inhabitants whose portraits express their kindness and modesty. She walks in the narrow streets passing by cafés to highlight that the place itself and its people are the real 'pulse' of the city who go about their daily struggles to make a living, yet they never abandon their humanity even under harsh economic circumstances. Hence, the title of the song becomes meaningful: the singer is in love with her country and its people. Islam Ali's love song 'Qahwa Baladi' uses a similar motif about the café when he asks his beloved to fill his world with laughter and joy similar to people's loud chats at the cafés. For him, this is a sign of life and social intimacy.[37]

Moreover, Hamza Namira's introductory song to the FM programme '3alahwa' (At the café) shares the same theme with the above two songs by reiterating that the café is the place where stories are told and where people socialize and become friends.[38] Cafés and their walls have come to witness historical events, and they are like the people that inhabit them: intimate, friendly, modest and grass-roots. The song goes on to emphasize the uniqueness of the place that welcomes all types of people, and where one feels at home and is happy to chat about life. The café's atmosphere creates 'laughter, joy, and a hundred million conversations', and it is far from being a place where people only meet to kill time: 'At the café, there are people who sample the taste of homeland', as the song goes. These characteristics reflect the content of the radio programme itself whereby the presenter would invite guests (musicians and artists) to feel at home and 'chat' about their life and work similar to friends who meet at the *ahwa* and share their stories. Indeed, these elements echo similar sentiments expressed by our interviewee Khalil, the musician, who said:

> I like to be amongst people and the *ahwa* certainly allows me this space. I see very interesting characters at the cafés. I can say that I find myself at the *ahwa*, with different people around. Life with its routines can take you away easily from joy, and the café for me is a way to connect with the people and enjoy their company. It's a 'breathing space'. The main characteristic of the *ahwa* is that it opens onto the street, so you are immediately with the people … you hear their jokes, you see the elderly sitting there and you can talk to them, and you see ordinary people going about their ordinary life. This is the real Egypt and I love it. In a nutshell, the *ahwa* for me is a doorstep that takes you into life. When you sit at the café, you feel the people's pulse.

Conclusion

This chapter has demonstrated that historically the café culture has been closely intertwined with music and poetry performances by popular singers and poets, as well as the production of resistance songs most notably as highlighted through the experience of the Canal Zone cities in their struggle against foreign invasions. Most of these performances used the Egyptian vernacular language rather than the standard Arabic to connect with ordinary audiences from all spheres of life, who found within the café social space a sense of collective joy. The café has been associated with the entertainment industry in the big cities since the late eighteenth century. This industry has defined the trajectory of many popular performers, including the iconic poet Bayram al-Tounsi; singers who became famous later on in the twentieth century such as Mounira al-Mahdiyya and Umm Kulthoum; and theatre legends such as Fatima (Rosa) Alyoussef. The theme of coffee and coffeehouse has been displayed in a significant repertoire of songs that have underscored expressions of love and romance, close friendships, and passion for the country and its people. Our research has pointed to the important concept of how the traditional café has created what some scholars refer to as a 'music scene' whereby the artist, audience and the spatial composition of the place create a collective social experience that ties them and leads to an inspiring process of the production, circulation and consumption of cultural forms. With the breakout of the January 2011 revolution, several singers who have taken part in it have revived the theme of coffeehouse mainly due to the enormous role that this urban place has played during the revolutionary momentum when cafés welcomed and embraced the political dynamics which were being shaped by the protestors on the streets with their huge numbers. In the next and final chapter, these themes will be expanded further through the presentation of a photo-story where our interviewees narrate their experiences of coffeehouses, and what the place itself means to them and to the cities they inhabit or have visited.

7

Pictures, voices and narratives of coffeehouses

Introduction

This chapter aims to present a photo-story based on eleven pictures of coffeehouses in Cairo and Alexandria specifically produced for this volume by the Egyptian photographer Adel Wassily. The pictures are accompanied by narratives/testimonies/stories which resulted from extended interviews with six residents of Cairo who shared with us their thoughts and experiences about urbanity and café life and what it means to them. We include these narratives as we transcribed and translated them from the Arabic original (except for Michael's testimony, which he wrote in English). We use pseudonyms to protect the identity of the interviewees. We only reveal their age, gender and profession. We have opted to include these voices as they told us the story of the coffeehouse through their own colloquial expressions because we did not want to disrupt the flow of the narrative itself, its intimacy and impact. There are powerful sentiments and ideas expressed in these narratives as well as a wealth of quotidian detail, and we hope that the reader will find in them many revealing issues about the centrality of café culture within urban living in Egypt and its role in shaping the city and contributing to its vibrancy.

Despite the diversity of views displayed throughout the photo-story, the reader will also detect points of similarity which a number of interviewees have highlighted even though the interviews were conducted separately and the interviewees did not know one another. The most remarkable point which seems to be a commonality is the influence of the Cairo downtown cafés and coffeehouses in their experiences and the extent to which this particular area of the big city is historic and unique. We have discussed part of this history in previous chapters and have documented what several writers and artists have said about the downtown coffeehouses such as Café Riche, Zahrat al-Bustan and al-Horriyya. But in the following narratives, the reader will observe how ordinary Egyptians have experienced these coffeehouses, not only the 'intellectual' class.

Furthermore, our interviewees have spoken about how the cafés played a crucial role during and after the January 2011 revolution and the sense of collectiveness that the protestors felt while gathering at those cafés to discuss, debate and mobilize for the continuity of the revolutionary movement for change. Both women and men got together to plan for activities and demonstrations demanding the removal of the military apparatus from politics and handing the state institutions to a civilian governing council. So many plans and campaigns resulted from these gatherings at cafés and have shaped the political landscape since 2011.

The affordable prices of drinks and shisha at the *ahwa baladi* is another issue that our interviewees have shed light on, pointing to the fact that ordinary Egyptians have, in recent years, moved in increasing numbers to socialize at cafés due to inflation and their inability to pay for expensive drinks at up-market places like coffeeshop chains, restaurants or bars. As a result, the café has been described through their voices as a 'refuge', a 'breathing space' and a 'community' where they feel free of social and economic constraints. Indeed, their narratives map out to us many suburbs, streets and neighbourhoods in Cairo and Alexandria where they have forged life-long friendships and spent much of their time socializing or participating in cultural or political activities at the cafés. They also underscore their relationship with café owners and waiters, and how this specific network of sociability is resembled to a 'system' of relations that enriches understanding between people and fuels a collective sense of social responsibility. Perhaps the most crucial perception which is highlighted by the interviewees is that the *ahwa baladi* is where the 'real' Egypt is to be found.

When reading these narratives and stories, one can invoke once again Henri Lefebvre's concept of the production of social space because the Egyptian coffeehouse remains to be a significant case study which illustrates and reinforces this process perfectly.

Introducing the interviewees:

- Samir, blogger and political activist, in his late 40s (the interview was conducted in downtown Cairo on 6 May 2018).
- Tarek, journalist, in his late 40s (the interview was conducted in downtown Cairo on 10 May 2018).
- Marwa, psychotherapist, in her early 30s (the interview was conducted in Mohandissin, Cairo on 13 May 2018).
- Edward, engineer, in his mid-50s (the interview was conducted in downtown Cairo on 13 May 2018).
- Michael, human rights activist, in his early 30s (Michael sent to us his written testimony in English in January 2019).
- Khalil, musician and performer, in his early 50s (the interview was conducted in Dhaher, Cairo on 13 January 2019).

The interviews were all conducted by Dalia S. Mostafa.

I. The role of *ahwa* in shaping social and cultural relations and the unique centrality of the downtown *ahawi*

Edward: In *wist el balad* (downtown), the scene is different. This area is a breathing space for people who are interested in art, culture and politics, particularly the leftists. Transportation to and within downtown is much easier than other places, so people coming from different areas find it more feasible to meet in *wist el balad* (an in-between area). Thus, we find that the cafés there are an attractive space for these artists and writers who are coming from diverse areas in Cairo to meet and socialize and discuss issues of shared interests. The downtown area in Alexandria has a very similar role as in Cairo. Some of the Cairo downtown cafés like Riche (Plate 1) have come to develop a historical importance in literature, art and poetry. Highly sophisticated cultural and literary seminars and discussions have always taken place in some of these cafés. Also, whether in Cairo or Alexandria, it is easier for women and girls to mingle with friends at the downtown cafés. In many other parts of Cairo, women from low-income and marginalized sectors do not have this freedom. They do not have the financial means either to meet at the modern coffeeshops or at restaurants. So the downtown cafés serve as a breathing space for these women who like to smoke cigarettes and shisha there as well. They can converse with men as a normal thing to do … they are not worried for their reputation. Outside downtown, we see women sitting at cafés but usually would be accompanied by their husbands. Some cafés designate a certain area only for 'families'. In downtown, things are much more open than these traditions. Of course there are also the 'touristic' cafés in cities like Luxor, Aswan, Hurghada and others where women can visit, but this is a different concept from the downtown cafés. Also, people travelling from other governorates to Cairo to do business or meet friends or to attend cultural or political events, meet their Cairene friends at these cafés. For many who do not live in Cairo, the main place they know is downtown … so they arrive at the main Cairo railway station and then arrange to meet in downtown.

Samir: The Egyptian coffeehouse has a historical importance in both urban and rural areas, despite the fact that it is a 'masculine' space. For example, to this day, women are not allowed to sit at *ahwa* in rural areas. In cities like Cairo and Alexandria, there are cafés which are rather touristic and we find women there, or we see some women sitting at the *ahwa* as a 'cool' thing to do. But this is not an indication that the traditional *ahwa* is an integral part of their social life or a way to consolidate social relations. Since Egypt is a class society, and since masculinist culture dominates social relations, these aspects are also found in a space like the *ahwa*. In popular neighbourhoods (*ahiaa sha'biyya*), women still cannot sit at the café. Yet this is not the case when we look at many cafés in Cairo's downtown area, for example, or coffeehouses which have a touristic ambience like in Aswan or in a city like Alexandria where people go for the summer holidays. Thus, the masculine aspect of the *ahwa* is not obvious in such places, but this is also tied to particular 'seasons' like the summer holidays. This means that the *ahwa* is not yet a place where women have the freedom to sit at any time they like. This has not happened yet in our society.

Khalil: My feeling about the *ahwa* is that it is a place outside the home environment, an open space where you meet people and chat. For example, I was never really interested to go to the café to play backgammon or domino like other men do. For me, the café is a space where you can establish social relations. I quite like the various types of people who inhabit the café. It has a very vibrant atmosphere, a joke here and a humorous comment there … it is a cool place. When I go to the more modern or Westernized coffeeshops, I don't feel at home at all because the atmosphere is quite formal, but at the *ahwa*, people are far more spontaneous so you can feel the real Egypt. The *ahwa baladi* is a very Egyptian place. And by the way, I never had a problem at any *ahwa baladi* when I had female friends accompanying me there. Even outside the Cairo downtown area; in Shobra, for example, I used to meet my female friends without any kind of constraint. It's true that the café is more of a space for men, but if two people (a male and a female) are passing by and they decide to sit at a café, there won't be a problem. I agree that the café is a masculine space but it really also depends on the type of women who want to sit at the *ahwa*. If the woman is open-minded and likes to sit there no one will bother her. The café is related in our society to the concept of going out of the house, similar to going to the sports club for middle- and upper-class families. If the family is lower-middle class, the women tend to visit each other at home. What I mean to say is that the Egyptians do not go out into public spaces a lot; I think this is a characteristic of our society. For example, you rarely see people going to any public parks and enjoying a picnic.

Marwa: Today, we see so many young people sitting at the *ahwa*, thinking about ideas together and they have a lot of things to do. For example, they say to one another: let's meet at the *ahwa* to arrange to do an activity ... let's meet to go to a film together ... the cafés are more open and lively now not just as places where bored people go to spend some time; or maybe the *ahwa* accommodates both ... so you see older men sitting there playing backgammon, for example, and next to them you'd see groups of young people doing something different. The *ahwa* is a more open space now.

Since 2006 until maybe two years ago when I started getting busier with work, a large portion of my time was spent at the café because this was associated with being with my friends. The café was the place where we met to decide where to go or what to do next ... to go to the theatre or to the cinema, or to join the demonstration. It was our meeting place, where we sat, chatted and stayed until late at night. The *ahwa* as a place has no limitations since it doesn't close at night ... no one comes to pester you and ask about what you want to drink or eat, or to say they are about to close. It doesn't have these 'closed' parameters like other places. It was the place that I felt to which I belonged and which had an impact on me. Even though the *ahwa* might be facing restrictions nowadays, there are so many young people who still go and meet there. These young people shape their ideas and interests through meeting in groups at the *ahwa*.

Michael: The café in my childhood was still a taboo for a guy who grew up in a conservative religious family like mine. I was only allowed to pass by the *ahwa* but not to enter or meet friends there. For my family, the cafés were places only for inappropriate behaviours and lifestyle. Heavy insults with loud laughs and sounds coming out of some cafés were enough to convince me of my parents' opinion. I started to form a particular image of the figure who frequents those places: a person who has no work and nothing to do other than sexual experiences, drugs and fights with other desperate guys. In those places, girls and ladies were not allowed to sit, or at least this was not seen as appropriate behaviour. Then I entered university life and hence my eyes were widened to explore an expanded horizon of diversity, people from various cultures, backgrounds and lifestyles. I started to find out that respectable friends usually go to cafés. I started to go with them to the downtown cafés. I still remember the first time I told my parents that I'm heading to a coffeehouse with some friends. They were totally shocked! I had to explain that those people are respectable and that in the majority of cases they belong to a church meeting. I continued to go to cafés and to encounter more and more different people. Since that point, my social life has been enriched a lot with so many colours of friendships, and my heart has remained attached to this social place.

II. The affordable prices of traditional cafés and their intimate, open setting

Marwa: I started sitting at *ahwa baladi* in 2006 in Helwan when I was at the university (Helwan University) with my friends, and also in the downtown cafés (*ahawi wist el balad*). I started taking part in students' activities during the *Kefaya* movement. *Kefaya* began in 2004–5, and the campaign for change began to extend to the universities such as Cairo, Ain Shams and Helwan. I was one of the students who got involved in this movement and worked with the Youth for Change campaigners (*haraket shabab min agl al-taghyeer*) in bringing it to my university. We were a group of friends as well as colleagues working within this political movement, so our relations were also social and human. We used to eat together and drink coffee together. We were friends so we spoke about everything, politics, cinema, our studies and personal stuff. The cafés were places which welcomed us, especially the downtown ones. At that time, the main campus of the American University in Cairo (AUC) was still there, so many AUCians sat at those cafés. In downtown during those years (2005–7), there were many demonstrations taking place, in addition to the area's touristic attraction. This is why it was easier for us as young men and women to meet more often at the *wist el balad ahawi*. One of the main reasons which led us to sit at cafés was their low prices. I remember when I was at the university, I used to pay 75 piasters or one pound for a cup of tea. Coffee was for one pound or one and a quarter. If one of us smoked they used to buy loose cigarettes. We were from middle-class families who had limited income and we used our pocket money to pay for food, drink and transportation throughout the day … we used to spend most of the day outside. Our pocket money was little so we couldn't afford eating at restaurants … those were expensive for us. We also paid part of our pocket money on the political activities we did, so sitting at the café was a great option for us, and then we could eat cheap sandwiches of *foul* and *kebda* from the street vendors around the café. Meeting at the café was the easiest thing for us. Our male friends made acquaintance with the waiters of the cafés … some of those were not very welcoming to groups of us, men and women smoking and discussing politics; but other cafés were welcoming and we sat there easily. I would say that most university students choose to sit at the cafés because of their low prices. The financial factor plays a major role with regard to where you choose to sit. Some people, young people, choose to go to expensive places. For them, sitting at the café is not a conventional thing to do. But people like us, my group, we didn't have anything against the café culture … even some religious people do not find it against their morals to sit at the café.

What makes the *ahwa* special is the type of setting (*a'da*) itself. Sitting at the *ahwa* allows for more space … for example, if you are sitting at a restaurant, you will be sitting around a table with four or five people in a limited space. But at the *ahwa* there's more space for everyone … even if you are sitting with ten or fifteen people. There is certainly more intimacy at the *ahwa* … people

Figures 7.1 and 7.2 Two views of the outdoor Zahrat al-Bustan Café

(off Huda Shaarawi Street, downtown Cairo)

sit close to one another ... there are no pretences at the *ahwa* ... people are more spontaneous there and speak their mind. So there is definitely more freedom at the *ahwa* than in any other public space. There, I feel that relations are based on a collective spirit rather than an individualistic one, as people sit in groups together. We build a collective experience at the *ahwa*. This kind of collectiveness is not found in places like Starbucks and Cilantro or in the usual restaurants. For me personally, choosing a particular café has always depended on who the owner is and where my friends meet. My friends used to sit at Zahrat al-Bustan café (Figures 7.1 and 7.2), so I sat there with them. But there was another café whose owners were nicer and it was also cheaper, so we liked to sit there as well. It really depends on whether the café owner is a nice guy or not, or where your group of friends go. Another important characteristic of the *ahwa baladi* is that it is in 'open air' ... you sit outside in the open air and this doesn't cost anything. You wouldn't be paying for the air conditioners or taxes or any of the sort like in closed spaces.

Khalil: In fact, we (my university group) considered ourselves the real 'owners' of the downtown cafés. We were mostly concerned with music, art and culture in general so we moved across many of the downtown cafés. For example, we used to go a lot to El Borsa café even before its expansion on the new pedestrian passageway. We knew the old Borsa. We also went to a café in Abdeen, and to another one which was located next to the Ministry of Interior (on Sheikh Reihan Street). That one was a very nice café actually. Also, on the street where you find the Bab el Louq *souq* (market), there were a few cafés there. But there was one in particular which I liked; I think it was called the 'employees café' (*ahwet el mowazzafeen*). The most distinct quality of all these cafés we went to was their cheap prices. At that time, we were very poor university students, so the only place where we could afford to meet was the *ahwa*. But then after the *ahwa* starts becoming known and a bit commercial or touristic, we would move on. There were other cafés on Sherif Street, and there was one on Emad Elddin Street which I liked, but most of them have closed down now. Another one I used to like a lot was the Umm Kulthoum café on 26th July Street close to the Supreme Judicial House. We used to meet there, as every one of us also had their own preference for a certain café. So we just moved across several cafés with friends. I have been to so many cafés across Cairo and Giza in different areas. On Faysal Street in the 1980s, I used to meet with a group of musicians and we would listen to each other's musical pieces played on the *Oud* (lute). There was one famous *ahwa* which was more spacious where we could do this, and it was rather exclusive where groups of musicians and their friends met. I used to live in Giza at that time so this café was nearby. I've been to so many cafés outside Cairo too. I travelled a lot to Upper Egypt and sat at so many cafés during these travels. I went to all the cafés next to the train stations in the Upper Egyptian cities as well. Of course there, you see all different types of people.

Michael: A new world of politics, civil rights and arts has been unveiled to me at that beloved space, the *ahwa*. I understood that there is a whole world there, a real one. I found the people I always thought they were there, people who are mainly interested in drugs, sex and any other thing that would fill their emptiness; but I also encountered, for the first time, friends who are kind and not pretending to be perfect or even aspiring for perfectionism. At the *ahwa*, there was a place for everyone regardless of his moral standards or socioeconomic class. This rich environment has opened the opportunity for many to develop their skills and fields of interest. Politics and human rights conditions were discussed everywhere there. I started to understand the difference between the right and left wings of politics. Critical thinking had a space in each idea. Even religious and untouched taboo issues of the mainstream were debated there. News about the latest important music concerts and theatre performances were always present in our discussions. Some of these cultural and political events were organized at the cafés. That's why the downtown cafés were always targeted by the police. Activists who usually frequent the same cafés know the police spies well … sometimes these spies can be the guys who work at the cafés.

III. Coffeehouses and cafés as political spaces and their role during the 2011 revolution and its aftermath

Tarek: During the long sit-in of the Property Tax workers which took place in 2009, where they had gathered in Hussein Higazi Street where the cabinet building is located in downtown, we used to go to the *ahwa* there every evening. The protestors would gather there to write their demands and statements, discuss the impact of their sit-in on a daily basis and make decisions on what to do next. This *ahwa* came to be known among us as the 'Revolutionary Command Council' (*maglis qiyadat al-thawra!*) When one would ask where the meeting was to take place, we would say: at the revolutionary command council *ahwa*. Also later on, when the Tanta Kettan workers had their protest on the same street, they also met at the revolutionary command council *ahwa*. It is as if they were continuing the struggle which the property tax colleagues had started before them, at the same *ahwa*. In other words, the café as a social and political space played a primary role in the organization of the sit-in for both groups.

I also believe that the *ahwa* played a decisive and crucial role during the January 2011 revolution. Thus, it was not a coincidence that the crackdown from the regime targeted the *ahawi*, especially in the downtown area. The Ultras, for example, had their cafés, and other revolutionaries also had their cafés. The *ahawi* which were around Tahrir Square were meeting places for the revolutionaries. Café owners started getting orders from the authorities to inform on particular figures when they went to the *ahwa*. Specific groups were targeted. As they cracked down on political parties and labour unions, they have also cracked down on gatherings in public places. But I'd say that what they have succeeded to do in the downtown area is very difficult for them to do in other areas in Egypt. It's very difficult for them to conduct these direct attacks against loads of places around the country. What I mean is that in many *ahawi*, there will always be a minority of people who discuss politics, so the authorities cannot close down all of these places but will give orders to informants to monitor their activities or discussions. So this wide-scale crackdown, closing down places and arresting people sitting at *ahawi*, like what we've seen in downtown, cannot happen in other areas. Thus, the revolution has led to the *ahwa* being the main meeting place to mobilize and organize campaigns and so on.

Samir: I believe that some cafés have played a particular 'function' during certain periods of time. For example, there was a very important *ahwa* on 10th Street (*sharei 'ashara*) in Wayli called Sorour café. This *ahwa* used to be the main meeting place for all the friends and supporters of the leftist labour leader Mohammad Abdel Aziz Shaaban who was running for parliamentary elections in the early 1990s. He was extremely popular in that area and had a landslide victory in the elections. We all used to go to this *ahwa*, I mean my generation of the 1990s. We used to meet there not only to discuss politics but also to read poetry and attend literary seminars. We used to discuss the elections and the nominees would present their programmes there. In this way, in the last twenty or thirty years, there have been popular cafés which have played a political role in our lives such as Sorour café. This is from my own personal experience. Yet, since political debates and activities are concentrated in Cairo more than other cities, we find that the downtown cafés, where both young men and women meet, have played a large role in our political lives as well as the political life of the city itself. For so many years, these cafés have witnessed political debates take place, and also literary and cultural discussions. El Borsa café was one of these places that witnessed this kind of activity (political and cultural); and also a small café attached to the Townhouse Gallery and Rawabet Theatre called el Takʻeiba, where many artists and writers used to meet. Al Nadwa al-Thaqafiyya café was also a meeting place for many people who were involved in politics, but no longer plays this role, maybe because it is very narrow and located on a small street. Nowadays, I find some of the cafés on Champollion Street vibrant meeting places for journalists, writers and artists.

With the commencement of the 2011 January revolution, a new momentum took place around the downtown cafés. The revolutionaries became the main customers, involved in political discussions while taking a break from the *midan*. This again changed the downtown cafés to places where politics was discussed day and night. In my opinion, this was the main reason that the security apparatus started planting informers or spies (*mokhbireen*) in these cafés, arresting many revolutionaries, with the ultimate aim of closing them down completely specifically after the Rabʻa massacre in August 2013. But I'd also like to comment that the *ahwa* is certainly a reflection of what happens in the wider society. Our society is based on consumerist culture with all its distortions. This has impacted on the function of *ahwa* and in my opinion has turned it into something like a 'distortion' of its original function as a social and public space. There are only very few exceptions to this consumerist pattern of the *ahawi*.

Edward: As for the political role of *ahawi*, I'd say that since the 1919 revolution, this role has been rising continuously. But this role swings up and down according to the level of political repression prevalent during a particular period of time. For example, the cafés for the leftist groups were known, and also the '*mokhbireen*' who went to these cafés were known. Before the advent of mobile phones, we used to make telephone calls at the cafés, and of course those phone numbers were monitored ... there were about four or five cafés that we knew they were under surveillance by the *mokhbireen* all the time. During other periods, we knew of seven or eight cafés which were monitored ... what I mean is that the level of surveillance changes according to the degree of political repression.

During the 2011 revolution, things were very different because the revolution itself led to a completely new way of thinking. I believe that the revolution was successful in achieving many important things ... people were able to break so many barriers and became absolutely aware that they had the power to change things. In my view, this is the main success and achievement of the revolution, not that the revolutionaries did not take over political power. The regime in power now will need a full-on counter-revolution to be able to erase people's awareness of their collective power to change things on the ground. They won't be able to destroy this major achievement of the revolution. During the revolutionary momentum, the cafés turned into places for huge gatherings of people from all age, class and gender groups. Large groups would start the demonstrations by meeting first at the cafés and then proceed to the streets and squares. In this, there was no difference between men and women. Even the café owners did not think about whether the presence of women was acceptable or not. These were not the issues that occupied people's minds at the time. The presence of women was normal, natural and spontaneous. The 'conservative' café owner had no problem with this, nor did the 'conservative' girl or woman who was present there. The cafés turned into open places for large sectors of the population to gather during the revolution. They also turned into places where the demonstrators could take a rest during the day. Because people used to walk for miles and miles, so it was normal to stop at any *ahwa* on the way and ask to drink some water, for example. We have also seen how some cafés turned into temporary 'clinics' where the injured would be treated, or those who were suffering from tear gas. This happened on very short intervals because both the café owners and the demonstrators were afraid they would get arrested. We need to remember that many of the informal *ahawi* do not have a licence to be opened, and hence a lot of café owners have problems with the police and they want to keep a low profile by not attracting any attention, so their cafés wouldn't be closed down. So during the early days of the revolution, some café owners closed their places altogether, but those who opened their doors did not care much about the police or military. The cafés were open to everyone, which showed to what extent many social barriers do actually break down during revolutionary times. When things were tense and bloody on the streets and many protestors were followed by the police, some café owners hid these protestors in their cafés. This happened to me several times. The waiters would let me in and hide me inside. On one occasion, the security forces broke into the café and beat up the waiters so as to inform on the protestors, and arrested two of the waiters but even so the waiters refused to inform on us and that we were hiding inside.

Of course, in the aftermath of the revolution things went back to how they were before 2011. But why did this happen? I believe it's because the police became a constant threat to café owners once again … and also because the cafés did become places for political meetings during the revolution and the aftermath. As a result, they were targeted by the police. Sometimes, we saw how policemen dispersed groups of people sitting at the cafés when they thought they were having a political gathering. Café owners started to feel the pressure from the police to inform on these political groups. However, and because I sit at lots of cafés all the time, I can say that this only happened in exceptional cases. In fact, the waiters themselves used to warn political groups to leave the café so as not to get into trouble. These waiters and café owners didn't want to be harmed by the police or harm others, so they would simply ask the groups to leave. This is why my view is that the *ahawi* do indeed mirror our society. During the revolution, there were so many positive things happening, so the cafés mirrored this positive attitude. Today, as things have deteriorated very badly, the cafés also mirror this decline.

IV. Coffeehouses and cafés as 'breathing' personal spaces

Khalil: There was also al-Horriyya coffeehouse (Plate 2) in downtown where we would drink beer as well. It was easy to locate everyone there as it was the meeting place for so many people we knew. We would go there, have a beer (which was very cheap then) and meet the people we wanted to see. I think as we get older, our needs change. So nowadays I mostly go to the café which is close to my workplace. What I care most about in any café is to feel comfortable there. The service by the waiters is not a big concern for me because once they know you well they will get you exactly the drink you enjoy. So I like to establish a relationship with the place itself ... I like the quiet atmosphere of the *ahwa* where people are friendly. I don't like the loud and busy cafés as you would feel you're in the *souq*. I like to be among people and the café certainly allows me this space. I see very interesting characters at the cafés. I can say that I find myself at the *ahwa*, with different people around. Life with its routines can take you away easily from joy, and the café for me is a way to connect with the people and enjoy their company. It's a 'breathing space'.

For me personally, the two cafés which impacted me the most were al-Horriyya and al-Nadwa al-Thaqafiyya. I've established a friendly relation with the owners and waiters, so even if I don't go there often they would still welcome me warmly when I occasionally visit. I don't go to al-Horriyya as much now because of the heavy smoke (even though I myself smoke), but the smoke there is so thick and heavy and it impacts on my health. It's also become very loud. In fact, my generation of friends no longer go to Horriyya as much as we used to in the past. I still like to go to al-Nadwa al-Thaqafiyya because I like the shisha there a lot and they make very good coffee. I also go to Souq al-Hamidiyya café, which is located right next to al-Nadwa. So this is the triangle that I moved across for many years in downtown: Horriyya, Nadwa and Souq al-Hamidiyya.

Samir: With regard to the famous al-Horriyya coffeehouse, of course it played an important role historically as a social and cultural hub for many people. This is due to its large space and affordable prices, and the fact that it also has a bar. So its customers were varied between those who would go there for hot and soft drinks and others who go to drink beer, or both. For example, a customer would go during the day to have a shisha, tea or coffee, and in the evening would go there again to drink beer. Although it closed down for a number of years, it reopened and its prices are still affordable, or at least better than others.

Marwa: I feel that the types of coffeeshops like Cilantro have started to increase in number ... there are many of them now in the downtown area.

These coffeeshops provide their customers with shisha like the *ahwa* ... they allocate an outdoor space for the smokers ... Many customers who smoke the shisha in these places are women, as they don't sit at the *ahwa baladi*. This is more acceptable now. Some women smoke the shisha outdoors, and others smoke cigarettes indoors. I think this is a positive thing because it was not acceptable that much before. But this change happened before the 2011 revolution. I used to smoke since 2009; but we also moved in certain circles ... you would be within the circles who accepted this style of life. Outside your own circle, maybe things were not as acceptable. So if passers-by who didn't accept such a behaviour (like a woman smoking cigarettes) would throw a comment or spit on the floor, or do something that would show their annoyance. But nowadays, there is more freedom for women at cafés, for example all over Zamalek, and in Mohandissin and Nasr City ... This style of sitting and smoking at the café has begun to prevail amongst different classes, not only the middle classes.

I think that after the 2011 revolution, we started seeing restrictions on opening new cafés. Before and during the revolution, we didn't experience such restrictions. Nowadays, there are security restrictions on the cafés and the authorities closed down a number of them in the downtown area. Those who open new places, it's more like the 'coffeeshop' type ... the owners pay a lot of money when they open these places, and also their customers from amongst young people pay a lot of money for drinks and shisha. I really don't like these new places. For me, sitting at the *ahwa* is more comfortable and much nicer, to be sitting in the open air. And also the cost is affordable, which is important to me.

Edward: It is important to differentiate between the cafés in popular areas (including the *'ashwa'iyyat* or slum neighbourhoods), and the cafés in the downtown area. Also, the cafés in old *sha'bi* areas such as Sayyeda Zeinab and al-Hussein are considered nowadays to be 'touristic' rather than seen as a traditional *ahwa baladi*. In Greater Cairo, the population has grown enormously, so people who live in a particular neighbourhood do not want to go out of their area. Very few people would go outside their neighbourhoods for entertainment. I'm talking specifically about the middle classes and the lower-middle classes. These people have become accustomed to live close to their workplaces, close to their families and friends who live in the same area.

Their kids go to the school in the same area … so these new areas designed for the middle classes (not the luxurious compounds where the wealthy live) lack many of the basic services; there won't be a hospital nearby, for example. Many of the newly built places in Cairo have not taken into consideration the needs for certain services which the residents require. In these new areas, as well as in other traditionally middle-class areas like Hadayek el Qubba, Manshiyyet el Bakri, Masr wil Sudan, and even in places like Dokki and Agouza, the cafés have come to play a crucial social and economic role, and serve as a breathing space for many people. The flats which are built in these areas are very small and the number of people who live in the flat rarely find the personal space they need. Therefore, we find that the 'man of the house' spends most of the day outside. He goes back home only to eat and sleep. Other than that, most of his life is spent at the nearest *ahwa* to his home. At the *ahwa*, he meets his friends, or his work colleagues or customers. Anyone he wants to meet he asks them to come to the *ahwa*. At home, he doesn't have a work space or an office to meet his friends or colleagues. In this way, the café has turned into the space where these economic and social activities take place for most people from the middle classes in Greater Cairo. I know engineers who meet with their customers at the café … labourers do this all the time … but there are lawyers as well who meet their customers at the café because they do not have their own office space, or due to the small flats they live in. As their flats are tiny, there is also a level of poverty in which they live. Many men are very conservative and they wouldn't invite their work colleagues to visit them at home so as not to see their wives or daughters within such a tiny space. Thus, for most of the marginalised classes and many of the middle classes, they meet their friends and colleagues at the café and stay there chatting and entertaining themselves until late at night … life for them is the *ahwa*. Home is just for food, sleep and sex. The upper- and upper-middle classes have other places where they socialize or meet their work colleagues like sports clubs or their own offices.

V. The *ahwa* as a feature of urban living and socializing

Khalil: I would say that the *ahwa* has been an integral feature of the Egyptian city for many generations … everyone went to the *ahwa*, and I'm talking about my father's and grandfather's generations. My maternal grandfather was from Isma'iliyya, and I remember him going to the *ahwa* there all the time. I also love to watch football at the café, especially the European matches. I enjoy the atmosphere of watching football with others who support other European teams than mine because then we tease each other and I enjoy the jokes and laughter. I go to the café frequently (every other day) and yes you can say that it is part of my routine. It depends on where I am, but if I find a café while I'm passing by I would sit and have a drink. I enjoy discovering new cafés so much. I recently discovered one on Klot Beik Street. It has such a lovely architecture and I really liked it because you feel Old Cairo on that street. I kept watching the people who work on the street because it's a very working-class area. The *ahwa* gives you the chance to see people in real terms ... I sat there for an hour and only paid 5 Egyptian pounds, the cheapest I have paid in a long time. But more importantly, I saw there very kind and decent people. I've also been to the oldest *ahwa* in Egypt, which is located at the end of Mohammad Ali Street. I think its name is al-Matabi' al-Amiriyya. I enjoyed visiting it a lot.

Marwa: Another key collective activity which takes place at the café is around football ... people agree to meet at a particular café they like in order to watch the football as many *ahawi* nowadays have big screens for this purpose.

Groups who work in theatre sit at the downtown cafés ... people who attend films at Zawya cinema, for example, also sit at the cafés around it ... you see five or six people going together to sit at a particular café. Groups who are interested in cinema, they wouldn't be just discussing cinema but many other topics ... intimate relations, for example, or topics about art, poetry, music and so on. In recent years, many projects and relations were built around the downtown cafés. For example, how the Zawya project was opened specifically to encourage independent film-making. Those young people who support such projects as Zawya are found in downtown. A lot more people started working on these topics since the cinema house was opened. Many people meet by coincidence while doing these activities and then they start a new project together, very similar to what happened during the 2011 January Revolution ... many people met by mere coincidence and then started projects together. We met thousands of people during the revolution ... some of them departed but others have influenced us ... some people got together and started new projects in arts, cinema and politics as well.

Edward: I have always loved *ahawi* and I have my favourite ones of course. Over the years, I've moved to many *ahawi* around Cairo. In downtown, for some time my favourite coffeehouse was al-Horriyya. At different times there were others, and this was not just my own choice but also that of the group of friends whom I mingled with. For example, we used to go to al-Nadwa al-Thaqafiyya café in downtown, groups of men and women; but at some point the café owner told us that we shouldn't greet each other with kisses (between men and women), so we decided to leave the place altogether and sit somewhere else. Later on, the owner apologized to us for what he said, so we started going there again. The behaviour of café owners sometimes differs depending on how well they know you. For example, there are some cafés which have alcoholic drinks, but would not let a woman who is sitting on her own (if they don't know her) drink alcohol, mainly because they don't want others to bother her. But if they know her, the waiters themselves would ascertain that no one would bother her, like at al-Horriyya coffeehouse.

I've been to Paris, and the coffeehouses constitute a key part of city life there. But the concept of coffeehouse there is very different from here in Egypt. In Paris, you go to the coffeehouse to eat or drink coffee, you spend half an hour or an hour and then you leave. But here in Egypt, you live your day at the *ahwa* if you want ... sometimes you even leave your stuff there and then go back and carry on. In many cafés outside the downtown area, you don't pay your bill on a daily basis, but when you have the money to pay or when you have your salary. Each neighbourhood has its own *ahawi*, so people know each other and where each one lives. I have seen how people bond with their cafés until they die. For example, I know of café owners who would hold a funeral for one of their life-long customers when he dies. His friends would gather there and they would hold a memorial ceremony for him. I'd say that this kind of spirit has developed over so many years, which indicates that the Egyptians have contributed a unique historical dimension to our understanding of the *ahwa* as a social space.

Tarek: It's extremely difficult to imagine our cities without *ahawi*, or villages without *ahawi*! I don't really have a clear answer as to why researchers have not paid attention to the relationship between the *ahwa* and the people in our society, and that the café's role might increase or decrease in particular periods or change from one era to another, and many other points around

Figures 7.3 and 7.4 Two images of al-Fishawi Coffeehouse in the heart of Khan al-Khalili Bazaar

(Al Hussein, Old Cairo)

this question. But I believe that academic research around cultural issues in general is minimal in our society. There isn't much interest yet in this subject.

VI. The breakdown of gender and class barriers at cafés and coffeehouses

Khalil: In the 1980s, I used to visit the well-known singer Sheikh Imam in Ghouriyya (in Old Islamic Cairo) and meet with Mohammad Ali who worked with Imam. Ali took me to some cafés in very narrow alleyways, and they were so beautiful. I loved interacting with the people there and watching the way they communicated with one another and their intimate bodily gestures. This fills you with a sense of joy and fun, away from the harsh reality that these same people live in. I can say that through moving across so many cafés, I got to know the map of Cairo well. Being involved in leftist politics pushed me to visit new areas and where else would you meet people but at the *ahwa*? If I were to meet a comrade in Shobra for example, I would meet him at his café in the area where he lived ... if I was going to Helwan to meet other comrades, I would go to the café where they gathered, and so on.

    Marwa: In my personal experience, the more modern places like Costa and Cilantro are very different from the *ahwa baladi*. In these places, you can meet one or two people, or sit to read and study on your own. In contrast, the *ahwa baladi* on any pavement is related more to a sense of 'collectiveness'. You'll find ten or fifteen people sitting together and you can join them, and they speak freely without restrictions. The setting is different. This happened a lot during the demonstrations ... you would go to the *ahwa* to have a break and then you find yourself sitting among a big group of people, ten or twenty, and maybe you only know just one of them! This way you get to know new people, and new relations would be formed; friendships and personal relations would be built; or you begin to organize activities with new people. I believe that the cafés also link different groups to one another. For example, the group who were demonstrating would sit at one café; and then the group who are interested in cinema would be sitting close by; and another group who play music are sitting at a nearby café ... the people who are members of a particular political group sit here, another political group sit there or sit at this particular table ...

in this way, groups feel that they 'belong' to such and such *ahwa*. Places like Costa and Cilantro are very different from this setting … they are places for individuals who go to study on their own or meet a small group of friends, but they are not 'central' places where you meet a lot of people on a long-term basis and sit there for hours and hours.

Tarek: Interestingly, the economic crisis has led to more women being able to meet at *ahawi*. I see this in some places in Giza along Mourad Street, for example. Most of the customers of the *ahawi* on this street are women. This was not the case years ago. Or even if it existed, it was on a very small scale. Sitting at the cafés is a cheaper option for women as well than going somewhere else. Couples also meet at *ahawi*. I believe that our society has also changed, and there is more acceptance of women to sit at cafés. So it's both ways: on one hand, the economic crisis has led to more people choosing the *ahwa* as a cheaper option; and on the other hand, the society itself has changed.

In Sayyeda Zeinab, for example, you see many cafés where women are present. I've just been to one of these with my wife recently. Even single women sit at the cafés … some cafés designate a particular space only for families, and another for single individuals on their own, and so on. But by the end of the day, women's presence is visible at the *ahawi* … this was not the case before. In Manial, even though it is not a *mantiqa sha'biyya* (a popular area), women didn't use to sit at cafés. Manial is a little more conservative than other areas; but now we see women there sitting at cafés. And I am talking about *ahawi baladi*, not the modern chains of coffeeshops. Of course this latter type is a different matter … a closed space with air conditioners! It's a different atmosphere. I think the fact that more women nowadays can sit at *ahawi* is a very positive thing in our society because it breaks certain conventions. Of course there are still traditions and so on, but their presence in the public space has become acceptable.

Samir: There is no doubt that the *ahwa baladi* still plays a significant role in our cultural, political and social life. They continuously increase in numbers. This enormous increase really needs a study on its own to find out the reasons for this phenomenon. Even in rural areas, there are modern cafés as well, perhaps not as much as in the city, but they are present there too. Many political debates and cultural activities still take place at the *ahawi* in popular areas, despite the security issues. The *ahwa* is part of the fabric of society, and its dynamics change along with the change in the society itself. Everything which influences our society and social relations also in turn impacts on the *ahwa*. Nowadays, for example, as more people are drawn into following world football matches, the European Cup, the African Cup and other championships, many people who live in popular areas go to the *ahwa* to watch the football especially that they do not have at their homes all the satellite channels which air these matches. On the other hand, many men like to watch these matches collectively. This has also created a new dynamic for frequenting the café … to meet friends and watch the matches together. People in Egypt nowadays follow other international teams like Liverpool and Arsenal (not only the local ones as in the past), so there is always a lot of discussion about each one's favourite world team and players. This sense of collective sentiments is very much observed in the *ahawi* nowadays. For example, there is a very important phenomenon in this sphere which again needs a study on its own, that of the Ultras. These groups were formed in football stadiums; they are the customers of the third-class seats who really care about good football. They mainly come from popular areas, from poor neighbourhoods and just care about the good game and to encourage their teams. They do not have any other interests except for the game itself. With the breakout of the 2011 revolution, these groups played an important role in the movement for change. This is why the security apparatus targeted them and massacred many of them in Port Sa'id, and have persecuted a lot others since the Revolution. At the *ahwa*, we often see people fighting on which match to watch (what I call the fight over the TV remote control), like in homes when husbands and wives fight over whether to watch the match or the film!

VII. Cafés as a masculine space

Samir: Since we agree that the *ahwa baladi* is a masculine space par excellence, perhaps choosing a favourite *ahwa* could also be a way of 'compensating' for the crisis of masculinity some men suffer from in their workplaces. Most customers of cafés in popular areas have low-income, are semi-educated, live in poor housing conditions, possibly with no jobs, etc. So being at the café and treated like a 'pasha' can be flattering for their masculine identity. This is contrary to how the big *mo'allim* is treated! In fact the real mo'allim does not go to the *ahwa* because it is the *ahwa* that comes to him, if this makes sense! The café owner would take the shisha to the mo'allim where he sits. There is a hierarchy of prestige between the mo'allim and the ordinary customers ... the mo'allim is like someone who sits on a pedestal and the men who work for him would not dare to transcend this social distance. I feel that this kind of hierarchy is a way to show the prestige of the mo'allim which he might not find outside his own area ... a way of compensation as I said earlier. On the other hand, the *ahwa* is also like a safe haven for the low-income men who frequent it after a long day of work and to escape the small flats they live in. They go to the *ahwa* to relax and chill. They find comfort in meeting their friends there. But I believe that this is actually a reflection of how social and gender relations at home are suffering. If men find their comfort at the *ahwa* rather than at home, then there are certainly deep problems within familial relations. The patriarchal aspect here is not specifically that men go to the *ahwa* when they want to, but in the fact that they do not allow women to do the same or to have the same freedom of frequenting their favourite café. Women in popular areas get together in their own quarters when they visit each other, or meet at the doorsteps and chat, or go in groups to a nearby park to smell some fresh air and drink tea. In many cases, it is not even a park where they meet but a mere little island in between two streets with a couple of trees and grass in the middle ... they take their tea and *hummus el sham* with them and their young sons to guard them so no one would bother them.

Khalil: I think in the final analysis the *ahwa* is a masculine space. Yet you don't really see what is shown in Egyptian movies when a woman is passing by a café and men start flirting with her or throw comments at her. This doesn't happen in reality, and the *ahwa* is not the place where thugs sit like some films show. It's not like that at all. Actually, I enjoy the traditional cafés in Alexandria more, maybe because they are bigger and more spacious. For example, my favourite *ahwa* is al-Borsa al-Tigariyya (Figure 7.5 and Plate 4). Every time I go to Alex, I meet my friends there.

I think that the *ahwa* is more present in the life of craftsmen, estate agents (*samasra*) and businessmen, and is more related to their work life in general terms. These are the sectors whom you mostly come across at the cafés. They go to the café for work purposes. What I mean is that the café also has this

Figure 7.5 A view (outdoors) of al-Borsa al-Tigariyya Café
(Corniche, Alexandria)

central function within the work market, not just a place for entertainment and pleasure. For example, I would go to meet most of the estate agents at the cafés when I used to look for flats. You also find car dealers at the cafés.

Edward: I cannot imagine our cities without *maqahi* (the standard Arabic word for cafés as opposed to *ahawi* in the colloquial language). Also, the economic crisis has led more people to socialize at the *ahwa*. They don't know where else to go! It is the first and foremost daily breathing space for the low-income and middle classes. There are no longer any parks or affordable places by the Nile to sit at. This is why the *ahwa* continues to play even a greater role as the main place for socialization. Of course this mainly applies to men, but for Egyptian women, generally speaking, we cannot say that the *ahwa* is their breathing social space at all. I can say that only *some* cafés in downtown play this role for women. Yet, I must also say that mostly the women who sit at the cafés in downtown are those who are interested in cultural events or political debates. It is this sector of women whom you meet at the cafés in this area. In recent years, some women started to go to the more expensive coffeeshops mainly to smoke shisha. But in my opinion they go there while trying to keep a low profile as they know that their behaviour might be frowned upon. Thus, I can say that the cafés have not solved the issue of being a breathing space for the Egyptian woman until today.

VIII. Factors contributing to the popularity of *ahawi*

Tarek: The *ahawi* in Egypt have played an important role for two main reasons: firstly, the fact that political parties and cultural/literary gatherings are not usually open to the public … thus, people have had to find places where they could meet. These places have historically been either the mosque (worship places) or the *ahawi*. The *ahawi* have provided a solution for many years for political activists to meet and discuss politics, especially during the Emergency years (under Hosni Mubarak) and the absence of democratic spaces. In this way, the *ahwa* has always played a social and political role. With regard to its social function, we find that particular social groups would meet at the café, for example, in Manial there's a café where drivers meet. It is the meeting place for all taxi drivers where they discuss their problems and consolidate social relations with one another. At one point, this café resembled a 'trade union', where the drivers discussed what they should do about the rising prices, the cost of petrol, the competition between themselves (the white taxi drivers) and the Uber and Careem drivers. The cabs' owners would also go to this café to meet with the drivers, calculate the money they have earned each day and discuss other work-related issues. This café was truly their meeting place. This type of *ahawi* is found in many other trades, such as for *hirafiyyeen* (craftsmen), for commercial company workers and so on. The *ahwa* continues to play this socioeconomic role.

The second reason which further enhanced the role of the café in our society is the economic crisis. It is true that this crisis has made less people able to sit at the café, but at the same time the café is still the place where people pay lower prices. Gradually, we find that the interests of the customers who go to cafés change over time and in association with their social class. For example, whereas many middle-class people used to spend more time in sports clubs and places by the Nile, with the economic crisis and the rise in prices they

Figure 7.6 A view from inside of Sayyed Darwish Café

(Kom el Dikka, Alexandria)

started to go more often to the *ahwa* ... it has become like a refuge for those with a limited budget. The economic crisis has surely led to the increase in opening a lot more cafés nowadays. This increase is also related to the problem of unemployment. We have a huge sector (around 10 million) of young people, new graduates from universities and academic institutes who do not have a job. These kids need somewhere to go to ... In Manial, we used to have maybe four or five cafés ... now we have not less than fifty cafés! The *ahawi* have expanded enormously, and more customers are amongst young people. We have of course cafés for the retired people (*ahwet al-ma'ashat*), but a lot more cafés are meeting places for *shabab* (young people). That's also why the café business is one of the most successful in Egypt today.

Samir: In the more Westernised coffeeshops (like Costa, for example), we don't really find all the drinks which the *ahwa baladi* offers to its customers. Places like Costa are specialized in particular types of coffee and tea, but they do not have traditional drinks like *qerfa* or *sahlab* which constitute some of the main drinks in the *ahwa baladi*. Some of these new chains of cafés do not offer shisha either, which is the main and basic activity at any traditional *ahwa*. In this way, we see how these new coffeeshops have taken the concept of the traditional *ahwa* in a different direction. They are certainly more modern spaces and suitable for the social class of people who frequent them, or places where there are both smoking and non-smoking areas and so on. This model is very different from the traditional *ahwa*. Originally, the *ahwa* is a place that offers shisha primarily, and other drinks. If there is no shisha, then it is not an *ahwa* ... it could be something else or we can call it something else, like a cafeteria, but not an *ahwa*. In my experience, one chooses his favourite *ahwa* according to how he prefers his drinks or the type of shisha he likes. At the *ahwa*, one likes to have his favourite drinks. For example, he can ask for the specific coffee bean he likes (*'ayez el bonn bita'i or 'ayez ahwiti*). One might have his own coffee kept at the café and would ask for it when he goes there. Or he would ask for the specific tobacco he likes for his shisha. He would have got on well with the café owner and waiter, so they know his preferred drinks even without asking for them. This is how the 'regular' customer is treated, as someone who is integral to the *ahwa*, unlike the 'passer-by' customer who comes once or twice and never goes back. One might also find his favourite *ahwa* because it is close to his workplace or to his home. All these are factors which determine how we choose our favourite or 'my own ahwa' (*el ahwa bita'ti*). It is the place where I like to sit … it has a sense of feeling at home surrounded by the people you like … a sense of collectiveness. There is also a sense of feeling 'favoured' by the waiter or the café owner … they know when to get me my drink or shisha … I don't have to ask for what I want because they know my routine … and so on. Also, how they would call you 'ya basha' (pasha) … there is the fun aspect of being at a place that feels like home.

IX. Café culture and gender dynamics

Marwa: I would say that there are still a lot of conventional ideas against women sitting at traditional cafés, especially outside Cairo. Alexandria is ok, it's like Cairo, particularly the Raml area. It's an open city, so people can dress the way they like and sit where they like. But if you travel to other places in Egypt, like Mansoura, for example, or to a rural area, you won't find this kind of openness. There, you see more women going to places like McDonald's and Kentucky, and different coffeeshops in the towns but not to the *ahawi*. In Alexandria, things are more acceptable for women to do openly because of the touristic nature of the city. In Cairo's downtown, it's the place where many demonstrations have taken place in the early years of 2000s, which was not the case in previous decades. Also, because people were used to the existence of the AUC there, they got used to seeing how young women dressed and how they looked and behaved.

In a place like Sayyeda Zeinab in Cairo, even though it's a popular area, it is acceptable for women to sit at the *ahawi*. In urban popular areas, women have more freedom than in rural areas or in conservative towns outside the big cities. In Sayyeda, mainly because of the annual *Moulid* (religious festival), many women do things related to this festival so they sit and meet at the *ahwa*. These women are not from the middle classes but rather from low-income sectors, *sha'bi* classes. But because of the Moulid's characteristics of being open for everyone from different age groups and classes, many women there sit at the *ahwa*. More things are acceptable nowadays, but it does depend on the nature of the place and what people do there. Many things are acceptable in Sayyeda because a lot of women and men work for the Moulid and they even stay overnight on the streets together. It is acceptable there for women to eat from the street vendors, sit at the *ahwa* and smoke cigarettes and shisha in the open.

Edward: Of course, the *ahwa* expresses the culture of the streets, and hence it can reflect what is happening in the society as a whole in terms of social and gender relations or how people think about society and politics and about issues of social justice, for example. I think that the *ahwa* is an important 'barometre' of what is happening in the society. I repeat: the Egyptian society is conservative. The rise of Islamic groups and political Islam, or even the present regime that is 'Islamized' in a way that manifests itself in the laws they issue (following a Salafi agenda) in my opinion, indicate that the society is getting even more conservative. The present regime is more Islamized than the previous Muslim Brotherhood regime. The permeation of Islamic groups within the society and social networks has been very strong for decades, in addition to the influence of Wahhabism and the Saudi regime in Egypt and those Egyptians who used to work in Saudi Arabia and have come back with the 'culture' of Wahhabism. All of these developments are against the liberation of women in our society. These groups look at women as inferior, and this applies to both low-income and middle classes. So of course they wouldn't agree that women would mingle with men at the *ahwa*.

Michael: Today, the café is the 'meeting point' for me and my friends. It's the point where we gather before going to do any other activity, and after arrival from work. It's where we eat, drink and watch our favourite matches. It's the melting pot for all our thoughts, plans, and dreams.

8

Conclusion: The Egyptian coffeehouse as a marker of collective identity

Throughout our exploration of café culture in this volume, one fact has become clear: for those who want to have a deeper understanding of contemporary Egyptian urbanity and social relations at the grass-roots level, their starting point should be the space of *ahwa baladi*. Our aim has been to underscore the centrality of the Egyptian coffeehouse since its early inception in the sixteenth century to the present time as a marker of a collective sense of belonging and identity closely related to what we can refer to (broadly speaking) as an 'Egyptianness' of a sort. Henri Lefebvre's work *The Production of Space* (1991) has informed to a great degree our analysis of the *ahwa* as a 'concrete place' and an energetic 'social space' where multiple ideas about the production and development of social relations in urban settings can be located. Indeed, we feel that this volume has added a new dimension to Lefebvre's theory in this regard.

Furthermore, Asef Bayat's notion of the city-inside-out and the visible presence of the 'subaltern' population on the streets and squares while taking their daily routines onto public spaces like the coffeehouse, has also helped to enrich our discussion of the historical, political, cultural and economic aspects of the Egyptian coffeehouse. We have tested the core of Lefebvre and Bayat's concepts in a diverse range of literary, cinematic and musical works through different eras in Egypt's modern period of the twentieth century. Our argument in Chapter 2 about the history of coffeehouses as an in-between place filling the space between the private and public has underlined the important fact about how café culture started in Egypt on the hands of the popular classes before the advent of the elite groups into this sphere. History has also shown us how the coffeehouse was associated since its beginnings with male gatherings who wanted to discuss new ideas, leading in a number of decisive periods to revolt and revolution.

From their earliest days, coffeeshops were loci of popular culture, whether in the form of popular spiritual practices such as the *dhikr* gatherings of the Sufis or sites for narratives of popular epics and vernacular poetry or, more recently, sites for watching television dramas and televised football matches. That intimate link between the coffeehouse as a site of socialization and a site of acculturation has informed most of the chapters of this book. These various intricately connected roles that coffeehouses play in the lives of many Egyptians almost naturally have led to their depiction in fiction, cinema and music. From the master novelist Naguib Mahfouz to directors such as Salah Abu Seif, authors and artists have used the space of the coffeehouse both as a microcosm of Egyptian society and as a reflection of some of the activities at play in society. In the coffeehouse, relations of power are played out and the city comes inside out.

Chapter 7 has brought into focus a 'narrative' about real-life perceptions, sentiments and experiences of the café culture through the lens of six residents of Cairo who shared with us their ideas and feelings about their favourite coffeehouses in Cairo and Alexandria. Through the voices of our interviewees we can better understand the position of coffeehouses in the social scene, and appreciate its depiction in literary and artistic works. One crucial point made by these voices is how the *ahwa baladi* mirrors the larger society, a metaphor which we have also investigated in some literary works by renowned writers like Mahfouz, Ibrahim Aslan and Gamal al-Ghitani. As one of our interviewees (Samir) said: 'The *ahwa* is part of the fabric of society, and its dynamics change along with the change in the society itself.' Indeed, it is not even conceivable to imagine the Egyptian city or village without *ahawi*. Interviewees who refer to the role of a person's favourite *ahwa*, their local hangout, allow us a glimpse into how the space plays a role in the formation and production of social identity. Which coffeeshop a person frequents, and whether it is a local neighbourhood *ahwa baladi* or a branch of a chain, is a social and political statement that people make and that marks their identities. It carries within it statements about class and attitudes about gender and politics. It is a form of indirect political and cultural expression that becomes precious especially when other political forms of expression are not readily available.

Another significant concept that we have developed in this volume is how the coffeehouse is not only a place for people with ideas but also so inclusive and diverse to the point that our interviewees have repeatedly said that it is 'where the real Egypt is to be found'. The concept of the coffeeshop as a best place to get the pulse of the nation is one that is echoed in both the practice of ruling authorities who at least since the nineteenth century relied on reports of informants placed at coffeeshops to gauge public opinion, as well as in the narratives of authors and film-makers who depicted coffeeshops in their works. We have demonstrated that the *ahwa* (for men in particular) serves as an extension of the home and work space, where they feel comfortable and where they belong socially. It is a space where they fraternize, exchange news and chats, watch football, find work through acquaintances, do business deals or mobilize for political change. In literature and cinema, as in real life, we have seen how many demonstrations and revolts started at the doorsteps of *ahawi*. Another interviewee (Edward) has pointed out: 'Of course, the *ahwa* expresses the culture of the streets, and hence it can reflect what is happening in the society as a whole in terms of social and gender relations or how people think about society and politics.' He resembled the *ahwa* to a 'barometre' that tests what is transpiring in society. Michael, on the other hand, has described the *ahwa* as a 'melting pot' of people and ideas. This social vibrancy has also granted authors various possibilities to use the coffeehouse for dramatic effect. As a slice of public space that brings together people with degrees of diversity, the coffeehouse offers opportunities for characters and individuals to move beyond their narrow confines and interact with others.

That potential for interaction and diversity, the synergy that arises from people, often men, getting together, and discovering each other, has also carried within it latent subversive energy that is deemed dangerous by many. From its early introduction in the sixteenth century to more recent post-2011 upheavals, authorities have often been wary of the energy of men sitting at coffeeshops and have sought to control them, whether by banning coffee, closing down certain coffeeshops, placing informants and spies at coffeeshops or arresting activists known to frequent certain spots in particular. The potential danger at the place is another running theme in narratives of coffeehouses, albeit not always a pronounced one.

The Egyptians' strong bond with their favourite coffeehouses has grown even deeper in recent years due to their affordable prices at a time when the devaluation of the Egyptian pound and the sharp rise in prices of basic items (most notably, vegetables, electricity, petrol and gas) has impacted the middle- and low-income classes severely. Youth unemployment is another visible aspect of urban life in Egypt. Consequently, as our interviewees have illustrated, many Egyptians (including women) have found in the *ahwa baladi* a social space where they can afford to spend time with friends and to sit in the 'open air' with like-minded people. It is a form of affordable entertainment and a way to kill time in a public space that can be stifling at times. In Chapter 1, we have underlined the symbolism embedded in the act of placing tables and chairs outdoors for large numbers of customers (constantly seen, heard and felt) as possibly one way of reinforcing the presence of the people and making them visible on a daily basis on the streets. This image of taking over the streets and alleyways is very potent. The increased proliferation of the *ahwa baladi* in particular in Egyptian cities has created a social vivacity and a place for many people to go outside the home and work environments.

Our research has also depicted how the 2011 revolution and its aftermath has impacted café culture, especially those located in the downtown of Cairo and Alexandria. The revolution led to the inclusion of masses of women in public political protests, debates and mobilization. Much of this activity took place at cafés scattered around urban areas, most notably around Tahrir Square, the heart of downtown Cairo. Since that point in 2011, it was not possible for women to go back to pre-2011 time when many of them could not sit at cafés on the streets. It is indeed a turning point in Egyptian cities that the contemporary *ahwa baladi* has witnessed this transformation in gender structuring. One future interesting area of research should be television productions and drama and their changing depictions of coffeehouses. In an age when serialized drama is becoming the leading narrative genre, and when much entertainment is a product consumed individually, the public space and possibilities of coffeeshops are sure to be continuing to change and to be offering more insight into society. Finally, we argue that our contribution into this lively subject area has a great potential to open up further studies and new directions in research about coffeehouses throughout the Arab world and to set them in comparative analyses of café culture in other parts of the world.

Notes

1 The Egyptian coffeehouse and urban space

1 Henri Lefebvre, *The Production of Space*, D. Nicholson-Smith (trans.) (Oxford, 1991), p. 73.
2 Ibid., p. 20.
3 David Harvey, *Spaces of Global Capitalism* (London, 2006), p. 128.
4 David Harvey, afterword, in H. Lefebvre, *The Production of Space* (Oxford, 1991), p. 430.
5 Ibid.
6 Lefebvre, *The Production of Space*, p. 416.
7 See, for example: Anouk de Koning, 'Café Latte and Caesar Salad: Cosmopolitan Belonging in Cairo's Coffee Shops', in D. Singerman and P. Amar (eds), *Cairo Cosmopolitan: Politics, Culture, and Urban Space in the New Globalized Middle East* (Cairo, 2006), pp. 221–33.
8 David Harvey, 'Neoliberalism and the City', *Studies in Social Justice* 1/1 (2007), p. 2.
9 Mark Allen Peterson, *Connected in Cairo: Growing up Cosmopolitan in the Modern Middle East* (Bloomington, 2011), p. 141.
10 Ibid., p. 142.
11 Ibid.
12 Islam Ali, 'Qahwa baladi' [Café], 2014. Available at http://www.youtube.com/watch?v=vtnPQM0CYu0#t=250 (accessed 15 April 2019).
13 Haidy, 'Ahwa baladi' [Café/I love my country], 2011. Available at http://www.youtube.com/watch?v=wohkVPre5Vc (accessed 15 April 2019).
14 The word *ahwa* can be rendered as a noun in the Egyptian vernacular to mean 'café' and also as a verb in the standard language to mean 'I love'; while 'baladi' in the Egyptian vernacular means 'my nation' and also 'traditional or local'.
15 Hamza Namira, '3alAahwa' [At the café], 2012. *Nogoum FM*. Available at http://www.youtube.com/watch?v=dpCLPSfAcNI (accessed 15 April 2019).
16 See a short report on this initiative available at https://www.youtube.com/watch?v=fecRuzbTfyY (accessed 20 June 2019).
17 Tarek Osman, 'Stirring up a Revolution', BBC Radio 3 (9 June 2013). Available at http://www.bbc.co.uk/programmes/b02626dc (accessed 20 June 2019).

18 One of our interviewees (Michael) has spoken about this initiative that he took part in and how it helped him develop a better awareness of café culture in Cairo. He said the following:

> In November 2011, while sitting with some friends at a local café (*ahwa*) in downtown Cairo, I observed with joy the dynamic movement of the waiters. I was feeling happy for them while they were doing this multitasking job: shouting for new orders, serving the orders, and before anything else smiling and joking with their customers. I was delighted by their social spirit and sense of humour. I discussed with my friends that I wish to live this experience. In other words, I wanted to put myself in their shoes concretely. They were taken aback at first by my idea but they quickly encouraged me. We discussed how our families and friends would perceive this. We are in Egypt after all and it is not widely accepted in our society to do simple jobs like that. We started to feel a deeper cause for my idea, and hence we started an initiative that we called 'Work is no Shame!' We went immediately to the café owner and discussed the idea with him. At the beginning, he thought we were crazy, but then he welcomed it. On this same night, I wrote an article in the Egyptian vernacular describing who we were and what we were willing to do. I went to the café with the other participants in the initiative and for the first time I experienced work in another space. It was my turn to serve the customers and socialise, but also to wash a hell of a lot of cups!

19 Asef Bayat, 'Politics in the City-Inside-Out', *City & Society* 24/2 (2012), pp. 110–28.
20 Ibid., p. 113.
21 Ibid., p. 114.
22 David Sims, *Understanding Cairo: The Logic of a City out of Control* (Cairo, 2012), p. 4.
23 For example, see Aksel Tjora and Graham Scambler (eds), *Café Society* (New York, 2013).
24 Bayat, 'Politics in the City-Inside-Out', p. 114.
25 Ibid., pp. 119–20.
26 Ibid., p. 120.
27 Ibid.
28 Ibid., p. 123.
29 Ibid., p. 125 (emphasis added).
30 Sonallah Ibrahim and Jean Pierre Ribière, *Cairo from Edge to Edge* (Cairo: 1998), pp. 14–15.
31 Ibid., p. 15.

32 Ibid.

33 Jacquie Posey, 'Dissertation on Early 20th-Century Cairo Coffeehouses Leads
    Penn PhD Student to Egyptian and British Spy Reports' (19 June 2017).
    Available at https://news.upenn.edu/news/dissertation-early-20th-century-
    cairo-coffeehouses-leads-penn-phd-student-egyptian-and-british (accessed 22
    June 2019).

34 Ibid.

35 Judith Butler, 'Bodies in Alliance and the Politics of the Street', *EIPCP* (September
    2011). Available at http://eipcp.net/transversal/1011/butler/en (accessed 22
    June 2019).

36 Charles Tripp, *The Power and the People: Paths of Resistance in the Middle East*
    (Cambridge: 2013), p. 72.

37 Ibid., p. 73.

38 Ibid.

39 Ibid.

40 Ibid., pp. 72–3.

41 Ibid. p. 73.

42 Ibid.

2 Betwixt and between: The arrival of coffeeshops in Cairo as an urban phenomenon

1 'Abd al-Qadir ibn Muḥammad al-Anṣari al-Jaziri, *'Umdat al-safwa fi
   hall al-qahwa* [The Noble's Guide to the Permissibility of Coffee] (Paris,
   Bibliotheque nationale), MS Arabe 4590, fol. 14a. Available at https://gallica.
   bnf.fr/ark:/12148/btv1b10030553w/f13.image.r=arabe%204590 (accessed 21
   July 2019).

2 Ibid., fol. 14a.

3 Ralph S. Hattox, *Coffee and Coffeehouses: The Origins of a Social Beverage in the
   Middle East* (Seattle, 1985), pp. 18–19.

4 Al-Jaziri, *'Umdat al-safwa*, fol. 31b–32a.; Abdul-Karim Rafeq, 'The
   Socioeconomic and Political Implications of the Introduction of Coffee into
   Syria, 16th-18th Centuries', in M. Tuchscherer (ed.), *Le commerce du café: Avant
   l'ère des plantations colonials*. Cahier des annals islamologiques 20–2001 (Cairo,
   2001), p. 128.

5 Rafeq, 'The Socioeconomic and Political Implications of the Introduction of
   Coffee into Syria', p. 129.

6   For example: Najm al-Dīn al-Ġazzī, al-Kawākib as-sā'irat bi 'ayān al-mi'ah
    al-'āshira [The Revolving Planets of the Notables of the Tenth Century
    (AH)], vol. 3 (Beirut, 1997), p. 165, mentions a ban on drinking coffee in 961
    (AH)/1553 (CE).

7   Andreas Tietze, *Mustafa Ali's Description of Cairo of 1599, Text, Transliteration,
    Translation, Notes* (Vienna, 1975), p. 37.

8   Edward W. Lane, *An Account of the Manners and Customs of the Modern
    Egyptians* (London, 1860), p. 333.

9   al-Jaziri, *'Umdat al-safwa* fol. 9b.

10 Ibid., fol. 10a.

11 Ibid., fol. 11a.

12 Ibid., fol. 11b.

13 Ibid., fol. 12b.

14 Ibid., fol. 11a.

15 Hattox, *Coffee and Coffeehouses*, p. 45.

16 al-Jaziri, *'Umdat al-safwa*, fol. 31a–32b.

17 Hattox, *Coffee and Coffeehouses*, pp. 100–3.

18 Tietze, *Mustafa 'Ali's Description of Cairo*, p. 37.

19 Nelly Hanna, 'Coffee and Coffee Merchants in Cairo 1580–1630', in
    M. Tuchscherer (ed.), *Le commerce du café avant l'ère des plantations
    coloniales: espaces, réseaux, sociétés (XVe-XIXe siècle)* (Cairo, 2001), p. 95.

20 Rafeq, 'The Socioeconomic and Political Implications of the Introduction of
    Coffee into Syria', p. 131.

21 Hanna, 'Coffee and Coffee Merchants', pp. 92–4; Andre Raymond, *al-Hirafiyyun
    wa al-tujjar fi al-Qahira fi al-qarn al-thamin 'ashr (Artisans et commerçants au
    Caire au XVIIIe siècle)*, N. Ibrahim and B. Jamaluddin (trans.) (Cairo, 2005),
    pp. 174–80.

22 Paulina B. Lewicka, *Food and Foodways of Medieval Cairenes: Aspects of Life in
    an Islamic Metropolis of the Eastern Mediterranean* (Leiden, 2011), p. 339.

23 Hanna, 'Coffee and Coffee Merchants', p. 94.

24 Ibid., p. 96.

25 Ibid., pp. 96–7.

26 This is a term coined by Thomas Bauer and used by other Mamlukists as well.
    Thomas Bauer, 'Mamluk Literature: Misunderstandings and New Approaches',
    Mamluk Studies Review 9/2 (2005), pp. 110–11; Konrad Hirschler, *The Written
    Word in the Medieval Arabic Lands: A Social and Cultural History of Reading
    Practices* (Edinburgh, 2012).

27 Hirschler, *The Written Word*, pp. 32–70.

28 An excellent case study is of the manuscript by Ahmad ibn Budayr al-Hallaq
    by Dana Sajdi. Dana Sajdi, *The Barber of Damascus: Nouveau Literacy in the
    Eighteenth-Century Ottoman Levant* (Stanford, 2013).

29 Nelly Hanna, 'Culture in Ottoman Egypt', in M. W. Daly (ed.), *The Cambridge History of Egypt*, vol. 2 (Cambridge, 1998), p. 109.

30 Malcolm C. Lyons, *The Arabian Folk Epic: Heroic and Oral Story-Telling. Volume One: Introduction.* (Cambridge, 1995).

31 Lane, *Manners and Customs*, p. 391.

32 This is part of the discussion in Cemal Kafadar, 'How Dark Is the History of the Night, How Black the Story of Coffee, How Bitter the Tale of Love: The Changing Measure of Leisure and Pleasure in Early Modern Istanbul', in A. Öztürkmen (ed.), *Medieval and Early Modern Performance in the Eastern Mediterranean* (Turnhout, 2014), p. 254.

33 Ibid., pp. 259–60.

34 Tietze, *Mustafa Ali's Description of Cairo*, p. 34.

35 Kafadar, 'How Dark Is the History of the Night', pp. 259–60.

36 Ibid., p. 260.

37 Tietze, *Mustafa Ali's Description of Cairo*, p. 37.

38 Nasir Ahmad Ibrahim, 'Adab wa tuqus shurb al-qahwa fi al-Qahira al-'Uthmaniyya', *Annales islamologiques* [En ligne], 48-2 | 2014, mis en ligne le 27 août 2014, consulté le 11 août 2019. URL: http://journals.openedition.org/anisl/2019; DOI: 10.4000/anisl.2019.

39 Ali Çaksu, 'Janissary Coffee Houses in Late Eighteenth Century Istanbul', in D. Sajdi (ed.), *Ottoman Tulips, Ottoman Coffee: Leisure and Lifestyle in the Eighteenth Century* (London, 2014), pp. 117–32; Tietze, *Mustafa 'Ali's Description of Cairo*, p. 37.

40 Çaksu, 'Janissary Coffee Houses', p. 121.

41 Ibid., p. 128.

42 Cengiz Kırlı, 'Coffeehouses: Public Opinion in the Nineteenth Century Ottoman Empire', in A. Salvatore and D. F. Eickelman (eds), *Public Islam and the Common Good* (Leiden, 2004), p. 80.

43 Abdel Mon'eim Shemeis, *Qahawi al-Adab wal Fann fil Qahira* [The Coffeehouses of Literature and Art in Cairo] (Cairo, 1991), p. 61.

44 Ibid., p. 75.

45 Ibid., pp. 75, 93–4.

46 Ibid., p. 63.

47 Ibid., pp. 65–6.

48 Ibid., p. 66.

49 Ibid., p. 69.

50 Ibid., p. 73.

51 Ibid., p. 91.

52 See Albert Hourani, *Arabic Thought in the Liberal Age, 1798–1939* (Cambridge, 1983).

53 Shemeis, *Qahawi al-Adab wal Fann fil Qahira*, pp. 96–7.

54 Ibid., p. 23.

55 Ibid., p. 99.

56 The word *bar* was also used in modern Egyptian colloquial to refer to places where alcoholic drinks were served. Cafés in the cosmopolitan cities like Cairo and Alexandria which served both hot drinks like coffee as well as alcoholic beverages sometimes used the name 'bar'.

57 Shemeis, *Qahawi al-Adab wal Fann fil Qahira*, p. 100.

58 Ibid., pp. 102–3.

59 Ibid., p. 105.

60 'Ibrahim, Muhammad Hafiz (4 February 1871-12 July 1932)', in A. Goldschmidt, *Biographical Dictionary of Modern Egypt* (Boulder, 2004). Available at http://libproxy.aucegypt.edu:2048/login?url=https://search.credoreference.com/content/entry/bdmodegypt/ibrahim_muhammad_hafiz_4_february_1871_12_july_1932/0?institutionId=6166 (accessed 10 July 2019).

61 Shemeis, *Qahawi al-Adab wal Fann fil Qahira*, p. 111.

3 Locating the *ahwa* (café) in the work of Egyptian writers

1 See a photo of Café Riche (Plate 1).

2 Tarek Osman, 'Stirring Up a Revolution', *BBC Radio 3* (9 June 2013). Available at http://www.bbc.co.uk/programmes/b02626dc (accessed 20 June 2019).

3 Henri Lefebvre, *The Production of Space*, D. Nicholson-Smith (trans.) (Oxford, 1991), p. 86 (emphasis is in the original).

4 Ibid., p. 85 (emphasis is in the original).

5 Ibid., p. 86.

6 The full archive is available at http://www.matarmatar.net/threads/34371/ (accessed 28 January 2018).

7 See photos of al-Fishawi coffeehouse (Figures 7.3 and 7.4).

8 Gamal al-Ghitani, 'Katib wa makan' [A Writer and a Place] (May 2011) Available at http://www.matarmatar.net/threads/34371/ (accessed 28 January 2018). This story is also available on the Antologia blog: http://alantologia.com/blogs/3489/ (accessed 10 April 2019). (Quotes from the story are our translation.)

9 Gamal al-Ghitani, 'Al maqha wa sahibahu' [The Coffeehouse and Its Owner], in A. M. Galal (trans.), *Maqahi al-Sharq* [Coffeehouses of the East] (Cairo, 1991), pp. 129–38.

10 Al Ghitani, 'A Writer and a Place' (Our translation and emphasis added).

11 Sonallah Ibrahim and Jean Pierre Ribière, *Cairo from Edge to Edge* (Cairo, 1998), p. 15.

12 Ibid.

13   See photos of Zahrat al-Bustan café (Figures 7.1 and 7.2).

14   See a photo of Le Grillon restaurant and bar (Plate 3).

15   Ibrahim and Ribière, *Cairo from Edge to Edge*, pp. 15–16.

16   Interview with Ibrahim Daoud conducted by Dalia S. Mostafa (9 January 2019,
     Cairo).

17   Ibid.

18   Ibrahim Daoud, *al-Gaww al-'Amm* [The General Ambience] (Cairo, 2011).

19   Amgad Shafiq (dir.), 'Zahrat al-Bustan café', *Al Jazeera Documentary
     Channel* (14 July 2015). Available at https://www.youtube.com/
     watch?v=eV6zsFykj90&frags=pl%2Cwn (accessed 10 February 2019).

20   Mohammad al-Bisati, *Al Maqha al-Zujaji* [The Glass Coffeehouse] (Beirut, 1979).

21   Mustapha al-Dab', 'Al maqha fil riwaya al-Arabiyya' [The Coffeehouse in the
     Arabic Novel], *Wighat Nazar* 18 (July 2000), p. 4. (Quotes from the article are
     our translation.)

22   Ibid., p. 7.

23   Radwa Ashour, *Siraj* (Cairo, 1992); Ashour, *Siraaj: An Arab Tale*, B. Romaine
     (trans.) (Austin, 2007).

24   *Siraj*, p. 73. (Quotes from the novella are our translation.)

25   Ibid., p. 101.

26   Mahmoud al-Sa'dani, *Hikayat Qahwet Katkut* [The Tales of Katkut Café] (Cairo,
     2010). (Quotes from the book are our translation.)

27   Ibid., p. 5.

28   Ahmed Mourad, *1919* (Cairo, 2014). (Quotes from the novel are our translation.)

29   Mohammad Abdel Wahid, *Hara'iq al-Kalam: Maqahi al-Qahira* [Burning
     Words: Cairo's Coffeehouses] (Cairo, 2004), p. 238. (Quotes from the book are
     our translation.)

30   Ibid., p. 237.

31   Mourad, *1919*, p. 177.

32   Dina Heshmat, '*1919*: I'adat ta'rikh garei'a taftaqid ila rouh al-thawra' [*1919*: A
     Brave Re-Historicization Lacking a Revolutionary Soul], *Jadaliyya* (18 June
     2014). (Quotes from the article are our translation.)

33   Ibid.

34   Ibrahim Aslan, *Malik al-Hazin* (Beirut, 1992). The novel was published in an
     English translation in 2005 under the title *The Heron* (trans. Elliott Colla). It was
     also adapted to cinema in 1991 in a famous film entitled *al-Kitkat*, directed by
     Daoud Abdel Sayyed.

35   Zuzana Kratka, 'A View from the Banks of the Nile', *Banipal* 27 (Autumn/
     Winter 2006).

36   *Malik al-Hazin*, p. 49. (Quotes from the novel are our translation.)

37   Ibid., pp. 111–12.

38   Ibid., p. 112.

39 Al Dab', 'The Coffeehouse in the Arabic Novel', p. 21.

40 *Malik al-Hazin*, p. 152.

41 Bayat, 'Politics in the City-Inside-Out', pp. 110–28.

42 Ibid., p. 125.

43 Al Dab', 'The Coffeehouse in the Arabic Novel', p. 5.

4 The case of Naguib Mahfouz: Storyteller of the Egyptian coffeehouse

1 Sabry Hafez, introduction, in Naguib Mahfouz, *The Cairo Trilogy*, W. M. Hutchins et al. (trans.) (London, 2001), p. viii.

2 Ibid.

3 Win-chin Ouyang, 'Naguib Mahfouz', *Literary Encyclopedia online* (5 May 2011).

4 Gamal al-Ghitani, *The Cairo of Naguib Mahfouz*, Photographs by Britta Le Va. (Cairo, 1999), p. 15.

5 Ibid.

6 Gamal al-Ghitani, *Naguib Mahfouz Yatadhakkar* [Naguib Mahfouz Remembers] (Beirut: 1980).

7 Ibid., p. 5.

8 Al Ghitani, *The Cairo of Naguib Mahfouz*, pp. 7–8.

9 Naguib Mahfouz, *Khan al-Khalili* (Cairo, 2014). The novel was published in an English translation in 2008 under the same title (trans. Roger Allen). It was made into a film in 1967, directed by Atef Salem.

10 *Khan al-Khalili*, p. 49. (Quotes from the novel are our translation.)

11 Ibid., p. 56.

12 Ibid., p. 273.

13 Naguib Mahfouz, *Zoqaq al-Madaq* (Cairo, 2014). The novel was published in an English translation in 1966 under the title *Midaq Alley* (trans. Trevor Le Gassick). It was made into a film in 1963, directed by Hassan al-Imam.

14 Bayat, 'Politics in the City-Inside-Out', p. 123.

15 Gayatri C. Spivak, 'Can the Subaltern Speak?' in P. Williams and L. Chrisman (eds), *Colonial Discourse and Postcolonial Theory: A Reader* (New York, 1993), pp. 66–111.

16 In *The Cairo of Naguib Mahfouz*, Mahfouz is quoted to have said to al-Ghitani during one of their strolls in al-Gamaliyya quarter when they reached the actual Midaq Alley: 'I remember that there was only the coffeehouse in the alley', p. 16.

17 See *The Cairo of Naguib Mahfouz*, p. 16.

18 Mahfouz, *Midaq Alley*, p. 44. (Quotes from the novel are our translation.)

19 Ibid.

20 Hafez, introduction, p. xi.

21 Naguib Mahfouz. *Al Sukkariyya* (Cairo, 2015). The novel was published in an English translation in 1992 under the title *Sugar Street* (trans. William M. Hutchins and Angele B. Samaan). It was made into a film in 1967, also directed by Hassan al-Imam.

22 In *The Cairo of Naguib Mahfouz*, novelist Gamal al-Ghitani tells us that this café actually existed in the 1930s, but was later replaced by the residence of Princess Shewikar (p. 13).

23 Hafez, introduction, p. xviii. Hafez also presents an interesting analysis of the spatial shifts of the 'coffee hour' from one floor to another in al-Sayyed's household throughout the *Trilogy* as symbolic of the changing social atmosphere and politics of gender within it, pp. xix–xx.

24 Kamal's eldest brother.

25 Kamal's second brother who died as a martyr during the 1919 Revolution.

26 Naguib Mahfouz, *Sugar Street* (trans. William M. Hutchins and Angele B. Samaan) (London, 1994), p. 43.

27 Naguib Mahfouz, *Al Summan wal Kharif* (Cairo, 2012). The novel was published in an English translation in 1985 under the title *Autumn Quail* (trans. Roger Allen). It was made into a film in 1967, directed by Hossam Eldin Mostafa.

28 See a photo of Trianon coffeehouse located in the heart of downtown Alexandria (Plate 5).

29 Naguib Mahfouz, *Al Karnak* (Cairo, 2015). The novella was published in an English translation in 2007 under the title *Karnak Café* (trans. Roger Allen). It was made into a film in 1975, directed by Ali Badrakhan. Parts of the discussion of this work were published in an earlier book by Dalia Said Mostafa, *The Egyptian Military in Popular Culture: Context and Critique* (Palgrave, 2017).

30 Naguib Mahfouz, *Karnak Café*, R. Allen (trans.) (Cairo, 2007), p. 3.

31 Ibid., p. 12.

32 Trevor LeGassick, 'Mahfuz's *al-Karnak*: The Quiet Conscience of Nasir's Egypt Revealed', *Middle East Journal* 31/2 (Spring, 1977), pp. 211–12.

33 Naguib Mahfouz, *Qushtumur* (Cairo, 2006). The novel was published in an English translation in 2010 under the title *The Coffeehouse* (trans. Raymond Stock).

34 Qushtumur is a real café which Mahfouz himself frequented.

35 Naguib Mahfouz, *The Coffeehouse*, R. Stock (trans.) (Cairo, 2010), p. 1.

36 Ibid., p. 2.

37 Ibid., pp. 1–2.

38 Ibid., p. 142.

39 Ibid., p. 57.

40 Ibid., p. 69.

41 Ibid., p. 75.
42 Ibid., p. 124.

5 Multilayered representations of the coffeehouse in Egyptian cinema

1 Viola Shafik, *Arab Cinema: History and Cultural Identity* (Cairo, 2007), p. 2.
2 On this theme, see Salma Mubarak's book *al-Nass wal Soura: Al Cinema wal Adab fi Multaqa al-Turuq* [The Text and the Image: Meeting Points between Cinema and Literature] (Cairo, 2016).
3 Shafik, *Arab Cinema*, p. 10.
4 Ibid., p. 11.
5 Ibid., pp. 12–13.
6 Nezar AlSayyad, *Cinematic Urbanism: A History of the Modern from Reel to Real* (New York, 2006), p. 1.
7 Tony Fitzmaurice, 'Film and Urban Societies in a Global Context', in M. Shiel and T. Fitzmaurice (eds), *Cinema and the City: Film and Urban Societies in a Global Context* (Oxford, 2001), pp. 19–20 (emphasis is in original).
8 Mark Shiel, 'Cinema and the City in History and Theory', in M. Shiel and T. Fitzmaurice (eds), *Cinema and the City: Film and Urban Societies in a Global Context* (Oxford, 2001), p. 2.
9 Ibid., p. 1.
10 Ibid., pp. 5–6.
11 Henri Lefebvre, *The Production of Space*, D. Nicolson-Smith (trans.) (Oxford, 1991), p. 12.
12 James Williams, *Space and Being in Contemporary French Cinema* (Manchester, 2013), p. xi.
13 Ibid., p. 2.
14 Ibid., p. 3.
15 Ibid., p. 4.
16 'Qahwet Ba'ra' episode (in Arabic), Al Nahar TV (22 January 2017). Available at https://www.youtube.com/watch?v=sItUgM0qiYs (accessed 24 August 2018).
17 Ali Abdel Khaliq (dir.), *Garei al-Wuhoush* [Race of the Beasts] (Egypt: Hussein al-Sabbah Films, 1987).
18 See also this short documentary produced by Al Jazeera Documentary (in Arabic) where interviewees talk about their memories at Ba'ra café and Gallabo café which is famous among musicians and singers, also located in downtown Cairo. Available at https://www.youtube.com/watch?v=KUaBRrteCdo&frags=pl%2Cwn (accessed 24 August 2018).

19 Viola Shafik, *Popular Egyptian Cinema: Gender, Class, and Nation* (Cairo, 2007), p. 249.

20 Ibid.

21 Lefebvre, *The Production of Space.*

22 Niazi Mustapha (dir.), *Al Tout wal Nabbout* (The Mulberry and the Club) (Egypt: Guirguis Fawzi Films, 1986).

23 Ali Badrakhan (dir.), *Al Gou'* [Hunger] (Egypt: Egypt Video Cassette, 1986).

24 Hossam Elddin Mustapha (dir.), *Al Harafish* [The Harafish] (Egypt: Mohammed Fawzi Films, 1986).

25 Naguib Mahfouz, *The Harafish*. C. Cobham (trans.) (New York, 1995). In the middle ages, the *harafish* were part of the urban underworld of cities like Cairo. Some of their behaviour could be deemed subversive. The historical *futuwwa*, on the other hand, dates back to the Abbasid period, and as urban armed gangs are also connected with chivalry and honour in the collective consciousness. For more, see Brinner (1963) and Irwin (2004).

26 Ezz Elddin Zulfuqar (dir.), *Sharei' al-Hobb* [Love Street] (Egypt: Helmi Rafla Films, 1958).

27 Kamal Selim (dir.), *Al 'Azeema* [Determination] (Egypt: Studio Misr, 1939).

28 Shafik, *Arab Cinema*, p. 130.

29 Kamel al-Telmissany (dir.), *Al Souq al-Sowda* [Black Market] (Egypt: Misr Company for Acting and Cinema, 1945).

30 Hassan al-Imam (dir.), *Zoqaq al-Madaq* [Midaq Alley] (Egypt: Ramsis Naguib Films - Arab Company for Cinema, 1963).

31 Mubarak, *The Text and the Image*, pp. 35–45.

32 Shafik, *Arab Cinema*, p. 133.

33 Hussein Fawzi (dir.), *Baladi wi Khiffa* [Traditional and Sweet] (Egypt: Nahhas Films, 1950).

34 One of our interviewees, Samir (blogger and political activist), has provided this cogent comment on Umm Za'bal's representation in the film and other similar characters:

> It is true that we have seen in some films how women can be owners of cafés, but in my opinion this image reflects further on the 'masculine' nature of the *ahwa*. I mean that even if the woman is the café owner, this doesn't mean that she would allow women to frequent it ... on the contrary, it remains a male space. This character is usually represented as a replacement for her dead or absent husband (the original *mo'allim* of the *ahwa*), or if she has inherited the business from her father or husband (like in the film *Baladi wi Khiffa* or some roles by Tahiyya Carioca). Here, we find the woman behaving in a masculine way and even wearing a *galabiyya* (long gown) which resembles a male's attire. She speaks in the man's own language, and would usually be smoking shisha. She is the *mo'allima*, and her power is derived from her

'ownership' of the place. She might also be the owner of the whole building where the *ahwa* is located, so she is in control of the trajectories of people who live in the building as well. This *mo'allima* is transformed into a 'male'. She replaces her femininity with the masculinity of her absent father or husband. This representation in a film like *Baladi wi Khiffa* is different from another very superficial representation of a *mo'allima* in some of Nadia el Guindi's films for example. El Guindi tends to appear very strong at the start of the film but then she transforms into a sexualised character after she falls in love with the powerful master. It's as if when such a character wears the garb of the master and behaves like him it is like going through a 'mental exercise' that has nothing to do with the real world. Nothing changes in the real world, and the change that happens to the character is just an exercise on her part of how to turn into a *mo'allim* or to someone who is powerful. She would then try to hide her feminine side and her femaleness.

35 Hisham Abul Nasr (dir.), *Qahwet el Mawardi* [Mawardi Café] (Egypt: Hisham Abul Nasr Films, 1981).

36 Khayri Bishara (dir.), *Youm Morr, Youm Helw* [Sour Day, Good Day] (Egypt: Al Alamiyya for TV and Cinema - Hussein Kalla, 1988).

37 Daoud Abdel Sayyed (dir.), *Al Kitkat* [Kitkat] (Egypt: Al Alamiyya for TV and Cinema - Hussein Kalla, 1991).

38 Radwan al-Kashif (dir.), *Leih ya Banafseg* [Violet Flowers, Why?] (Egypt: Dana for Artistic Production and Distribution, 1993).

39 Asef Bayat, 'Un-Civil Society: The Politics of the "Informal People"', *Third World Quarterly* 18/1 (1997), p. 58.

40 Ibid.

41 Mahmoud Khairallah, *Barat Misr* [Egypt's Pubs] (Cairo, 2016), p. 63.

42 Saly Abu Shadi (dir.), 'Café Riche', Al Jazeera Documentary Channel (2 July 2015). Available at https://www.youtube.com/watch?v=HNNmcSuUnhw&frags=pl%2Cwn (accessed 30 August 2018).

43 In Chapter 3, we discussed how author Ahmed Mourad fictionalized the revolutionary role of Café Riche in his novel *1919*.

44 Ali Badrakhan (dir.), *Al Karnak* (Egypt: Leithi Films, 1975).

45 Atef Salem (dir.), *Khan al-Khalili* (Egypt: The General Egyptian Cinema Organisation, 1967).

46 Hassan al-Imam (dir.), *Qasr al-Shouq* [Palace of Desire] (Egypt: Helmi Rafla Films, 1967).

47 Hassan al-Imam (dir.), *Al Sukarriyya* [Sugar Street] (Egypt: Sobhi Farahat Films, 1973).

48 Salah Abu Seif (dir.), *Al Saqqa Mat* [The Water Carrier Is Dead] (Egypt and Tunisia: Misr International Film Company and the Tunisian Company for Cinematic Development and Production, 1977).

49 Sami al-Salamouni quoted in Hashim al-Nahhas, *Salah Abu Seif: Mohawarat Hashim al-Nahhas* [Salah Abu Seif: Conversations with Hashim al-Nahhas] (Cairo, 1996), p. 256.

50 Ibid., p. 196.

51 Writer Abdel Mon'eim Shemeis (1991) demonstrates in his book *Qahawi al-Adab wal Fann fil Qahira* [The Coffeehouses of Literature and Art in Cairo] that al-Afandiyya café did exist and was located near al-Azhar mosque. The word *afandiyya* in Arabic refers to men who used to adopt the Western dress (a full suit rather than the traditional *galabiyya* or long gown) and wear the Fez. This coffeehouse, according to Shemeis, was inhabited mainly by these men who were particularly interested in literature, but was also a meeting place for the religious Sheikhs (pp. 35–7).

52 Kamla Abu Zikri (dir.), *Malik wi Ketaba* [Heads & Tails] (Egypt: Al Batriq Company for Artistic Production, 2006).

53 See a photo of al-Horriyya coffeehouse (Plate 2).

6 Egyptian singers and performers: An integral relation to the coffeehouse

1 Abdel Mon'eim Shemeis, *Qahawi al-Adab wal Fann fil Qahira* [The Coffeehouses of Literature and Art in Cairo] (Cairo, 1991), pp. 26–34.

2 Ibid., p. 13.

3 Ibid., p. 24.

4 Ibid., pp. 19–20.

5 'Urghul Bayram al-Tounsi', *Al Ahram* newspaper (in Arabic), 4 October 2014. However, the *mawwal*, although already well-established by the twelfth century as a non-classical Arabic rhymed verse form associated with folk poetry, it grew more popular and developed into multi-rhyme compositions in the early modern period. For more, see Cachia (*Encyclopaedia of Islam*, 2nd edn).

6 Shemeis, pp. 23–4.

7 Ibid., p. 25.

8 Ibid., p. 29.

9 Ibid., pp. 36–7.

10 Ibid., p. 57.

11 Ibid., pp. 59–60.

12 Ibid., pp. 47–8.

13 S. Oakes and G. Warnaby analyse how live outdoor music of different genres contributes to an overall urban 'servicescape' capable of transforming perceptions of urban environments. See Steve Oakes and Gary Warnaby, 'Conceptualizing the

Management and Consumption of Live Music in Urban Space', *Marketing Theory* 11/4 (2011), p. 405.

14 Ibid., p. 407.

15 Oakes and Warnaby introduce this idea of 'demystifying high art' in their discussion of outdoor jazz concerts in Manchester, p. 410.

16 Amgad Shafiq (dir.), 'Zahret el Bustan Café', Al Jazeera Documentary Channel (14 July 2015). Available at https://www.youtube.com/watch?v=eV6zsFykj90&frags=pl%2Cwn (accessed 10 February 2019).

17 See a photo of the café (Figure 7.6).

18 Sherif Hilal (dir.), 'Sayyed Darwish Café', Al Jazeera Documentary Channel (29 June 2015). Available at https://www.youtube.com/watch?v=SxTRIgwdHg0&frags=pl%2Cwn (accessed 8 February 2019).

19 Christopher Driver and Andy Bennett, 'Music Scenes, Space and the Body', *Cultural Sociology* 9/1 (2015), p. 99.

20 Ibid., p. 100.

21 Will Straw, 'Systems of Articulation, Logic of Change: Communities and Scenes in Popular Music', *Cultural Studies* 5/3 (1991), p. 373.

22 Khalil, interview with Dalia S. Mostafa (13 January 2019, Cairo).

23 Asmahan, 'Ana Ahwa' [I am in Love], 1944. Available at https://www.youtube.com/watch?v=oqh60M05Vmo&frags=pl%2Cwn (accessed 20 January 2018).

24 See al-Gizawi performing the song 'Itfaddal Gahwa' [Please come in and have some coffee] on a different occasion on the theatre stage, available at https://www.youtube.com/watch?v=hDWxOF9vF_o&frags=pl%2Cwn (accessed 20 January 2018).

25 Ahmed Munib, 'Talab al-ahwa wi ma shribhash' [He asked for coffee and didn't drink it]. Available at https://www.youtube.com/watch?v=bIa_gfffJmk&frags=pl%2Cwn (accessed 20 January 2018).

26 See this brief article in Arabic about the programme. Available at https://www.almasryalyoum.com/news/details/767352 (accessed 14 June 2020).

27 For example, see these two episodes of the programme with Sheikh Yassin al-Tuhami and Rayyes Mitqal: https://www.youtube.com/watch?v=VB8nWNQtwdE&frags=pl%2Cwn and https://www.youtube.com/watch?v=8K00gPFGpZU&frags=pl%2Cwn (accessed 14 June 2020).

28 See the episode on YouTube. Available at https://www.youtube.com/watch?v=x0lSJN6DdlQ&frags=pl%2Cwn (accessed 14 June 2020).

29 See the episode on YouTube. Available at https://www.youtube.com/watch?v=dLjO0qevo2g&frags=pl%2Cwn (accessed 14 June 2020).

30 Dwight Reynolds. *Arab Folklore: A Handbook* (Connecticut, 2007), pp. 146–50.

31 More information about the traditional instruments of the Canal Zone cities and their history of political resistance in the twentieth century can be traced through

El Mastaba Centre for Egyptian Folk Music webpage. Available at https://www. el-mastaba.org/home.html (accessed 14 June 2020).

32 Sherif Hilal (dir.), 'Borset al-Fallah Café', Al Jazeera Documentary Channel (1 July 2015). Available at https://www.youtube.com/watch?v=iIg_WBW71zs&frags=pl%2Cwn (accessed 30 August 2018).

33 Arab Lotfi (dir.), *Saba' Layali wi Subhiyya* [Seven Nights and a Dawn] (Egypt: Satellite Specialised Nile Channels, 1998).

34 Dalia S. Mostafa in conversation with Arab Lotfi, 28 June 2010.

35 The reader will find some reflections on these issues through the voices of our interviewees in Chapter 7.

36 Haidy, 'Ahwa Baladi' ['Café/I love my country'], 2011. Available at https://www. youtube.com/watch?v=wohkVPre5Vc (accessed 30 January 2019).

37 Islam Ali, 'Qahwa Baladi' ['Café'], 2014. Available at https://www.youtube.com/ watch?v=vtnPQM0CYu0&frags=pl%2Cwn (accessed 30 January 2019).

38 Hamza Namira, '3alahwa' ['At the café'], 2012. Available at https://www.youtube. com/watch?v=dpCLPSfAcNI (accessed 30 January 2019).

Bibliography

Publications

Abaza, Mona, 'Post January Revolution Cairo: Urban Wars and the Reshaping of Public Space', *Theory, Culture & Society* 31/7–8 (2014), pp. 163–83.

Abaza, Mona, 'Walls, Segregating Downtown Cairo and the Mohammed Mahmud Graffiti', *Theory, Culture & Society* 30/1 (2013), pp. 122–39.

'Abd al-Halim, 'Id, *Hikayat Maqahi al-Safwa wa al-Harafish* [The Tales of Elite and Harafish Coffeehouses] (Cairo: al-Hay'a al-'Amma li-Qusur al-Thaqafa, 2014).

Abdelrahman, Maha, *Egypt's Long Revolution: Protest Movements and Uprisings* (London: Routledge, 2014).

Abdelrahman, Maha, 'Policing Neoliberalism in Egypt: The Continuing Rise of the "Securocratic" State', *Third World Quarterly* 38/1 (2016), pp. 180–202.

Abdel Wahid, Mohammad, *Hara'iq al-Kalam: Maqahi al-Qahira* [Burning Words: Cairo's Coffeehouses] (Cairo: Maktabat al-Ussra, 2004).

AlSayyad, Nezar, *Cinematic Urbanism: A History of the Modern from Reel to Real* (New York: Routledge, 2006).

Ashour, Radwa, *Siraj* (Cairo: Dar al-Shorouq, 2014).

Ashour, Radwa, *Siraaj: An Arab Tale*, B. Romaine (trans.) (Austin: University of Texas Press, 2007).

Aslan, Ibrahim, *Malik al-Hazin* (Beirut: Dar al-Adab, 1992).

Aslan, Ibrahim, *The Heron*, E. Colla (trans.) (Cairo: American University in Cairo Press, 2005).

Bauer, Thomas, 'Mamluk Literature: Misunderstandings and New Approaches', *Mamluk Studies Review* 9/2 (2005), pp. 105–32.

Bayat, Asef, 'Un-Civil Society: The Politics of the "Informal People"', *Third World Quarterly* 18/1 (1997), pp. 53–72.

Bayat, Asef, 'Politics in the City-Inside-Out', *City & Society* 24/2 (2012), pp. 110–28.

al-Bisati, Mohammad, *Al Maqha al-Zujaji* [The Glass Coffeehouse] (Beirut: Dar Ibn Rushd, 1979).

Brinner, William M., 'The Significance of the Ḥarāfīsh and Their "Sultan"', *Journal of the Economic and Social History of the Orient* 6/2 (1963), pp. 190–215.

Butler, Judith, 'Bodies in Alliance and the Politics of the Street', *EIPCP* (September 2011). Available at http://eipcp.net/transversal/1011/butler/en (accessed 22 June 2017).

Cachia, P. and Ed., `Mawāliyā`, in P. Bearman et al. (eds), *Encyclopaedia of Islam, Second Edition*. Available at https://referenceworks.brillonline.com/entries/encyclopaedia-of-islam-2/mawaliya-COM_0712 (accessed 20 July 2020).

Çaksu, Ali, 'Janissary Coffee Houses in Late Eighteenth Century Istanbul', in D. Sajdi (ed.), *Ottoman Tulips, Ottoman Coffee: Leisure and Lifestyle in the Eighteenth Century* (London: I.B. Tauris, 2014), pp. 117–32.

al-Dab', Mustapha, 'Al Maqha fil Riwaya al-Arabiyya' [The Coffeehouse in the Arabic Novel], *Wighat Nazar* 18 (July 2000), pp. 1–24.

Daoud, Ibrahim, *al-Gaww al-'Amm* [The General Ambience] (Cairo: Dar Mirett, 2011).

Deboulet, Agnès, 'The Dictatorship of the Straight Line and the Myth of Social Disorder: Revisiting Informality in Cairo', in D. Singerman (ed.), *Cairo Contested: Governance, Urban Space, and Global Modernity* (Cairo: American University in Cairo Press, 2009), pp. 199–234.

De Koning, Anouk, 'Café Latte and Caesar Salad: Cosmopolitan Belonging in Cairo's Coffee Shops', in D. Singerman and P. Amar (eds), *Cairo Cosmopolitan: Politics, Culture, and Urban Space in the New Globalised Middle East* (Cairo: American University in Cairo Press, 2006), pp. 221–33.

Driver, Christopher, and Bennett, Andy, 'Music Scenes, Space and the Body', *Cultural Sociology* 9/1 (2015), pp. 99–115.

El-Mahdi, Rabab, and Marfleet, Philip (eds), *Egypt: The Moment of Change* (London: Zed Books, 2009).

'El Qahwa Baladi' Programme. Available at https://www.youtube.com/watch?v=fecRuzbTfyY (accessed 20 June 2017).

Fitzmaurice, Tony, 'Film and Urban Societies in a Global Context', in M. Shiel and T. Fitzmaurice (eds), *Cinema and the City: Film and Urban Societies in a Global Context* (Oxford: Blackwell, 2001), pp. 19–30.

al-Ghitani, Gamal, *The Cairo of Naguib Mahfouz*, Photographs by Britta Le Va (Cairo: American University in Cairo Press, 1999).

al-Ghitani, Gamal, 'Katib wa Makan' (A writer and a place) (May 2011). Available at http://www.matarmatar.net/threads/34371/ (Arabic) (accessed 28 January 2018). Also available at the *Antologia* blog: http://alantologia.com/blogs/3489/ (accessed 10 April 2019).

al-Ghitani, Gamal, 'Al Maqha wa Sahibahu' [The Coffeehouse and Its Owner], in A. M. Galal (trans.), *Maqahi al-Sharq* [Coffeehouses of the East] (Cairo: Mu'assassat Akhbar al-Youm, 1991), pp. 129–38.

al-Ghitani, Gamal, *Naguib Mahfouz Yatadhakkar* [Naguib Mahfouz Remembers] (Beirut: Dar al-Massira, 1980).

Goldschmidt, A., 'Ibrahim, Muhammad Hafiz (4 February 1871–12 July 1932)', in *Biographical Dictionary of Modern Egypt* (Boulder, CO: Lynne Rienner, 2004).

Hafez, Sabry, introduction, in Naguib Mahfouz, *The Cairo Trilogy*, W. M. Hutchins et al. (trans.) (London: Everyman's Library, 2001).

Hanna, Nelly, 'Coffee and Coffee Merchants in Cairo 1580–1630', in M. Tuchscherer (ed.), *Le commerce du café avant l'ère des plantations coloniales: Espaces, réseaux, sociétés (XVe-XIXe siècle)* (Cairo: Institut Français d'Archéologie Orientale, 2001), pp. 91–101.

Hanna, Nelly, 'Culture in Ottoman Egypt', in M. W. Daly (ed.), *The Cambridge History of Egypt*, vol. 2 (Cambridge: Cambridge University Press, 1998), pp. 87–112.

Harvey, David, 'Neoliberalism and the City', *Studies in Social Justice* 1/1 (2007), pp. 2–13.

Harvey, David, *Spaces of Global Capitalism* (London: Verso, 2006).

Hattox, Ralph S., *Coffee and Coffeehouses: The Origins of a Social Beverage in the Middle East* (Seattle: University of Washington Press, 1985).

Heshmat, Dina, '*1919*: I'adat ta'rikh garei'a taftaqid ila rouh al-thawra' [1919: A Brave Re-Historicisation Lacking a Revolutionary Soul], *Jadaliyya* (18 June 2014).

Hirschler, Konrad, *The Written Word in the Medieval Arabic Lands: A Social and Cultural History of Reading Practices* (Edinburgh: Edinburgh University Press, 2012).

Hourani, Albert, *Arabic Thought in the Liberal Age, 1798–1939* (Cambridge: Cambridge University Press, 1983).

Ibrahim, Nasir A., 'Adab wa tuqus shurb al-qahwa fi al-Qahira al-'Uthmaniyya' [Manners and Rituals of Drinking Coffee in Ottoman Egypt], *Annales islamologiques* [En ligne], 48-2 | 2014, mis en ligne le 27 août 2014, consulté le 11 août 2019. URL: http://journals.openedition.org/anisl/2019; DOI: 10.4000/anisl 2019.

Ibrahim, Sonallah, and Ribière, Jean Pierre, *Cairo from Edge to Edge* (Cairo: American University in Cairo Press, 1998).

Irwin, Robert, ' "Futuwwa": Chivalry and *Gangsterism* in Medieval Cairo', *Muqarnas* 21 (2004), pp. 161–70.

Ismail, Salwa, 'Authoritarian Government, Neoliberalism and Everyday Civilities in Egypt', *Third World Quarterly* 32/5 (2011), pp. 845–62.

al-Jazirī, 'Abd al-Qādir ibn Muḥammad al-Anṣārī, '*Umdat al-safwa fi hall al-qahwa* [The Noble's Guide to the Permissibility of Coffee] (Paris: Bibliotheque nationale

de France, MS Arabe 4590). Available at https://gallica.bnf.fr/ark:/12148/
   btv1b10030553w/f13.image.r=arabe%204590 (accessed 21 July 2019).

Kafadar, Cemal, 'How Dark Is the History of the Night, How Black the Story of Coffee,
   How Bitter the Tale of Love: The Changing Measure of Leisure and Pleasure in
   Early Modern Istanbul', in A. Öztürkmen (ed.), *Medieval and Early Modern
   Performance in the Eastern Mediterranean* (Turnhout: Brepols, 2014), pp. 243–69.

Khairallah, Mahmoud, *Barat Misr* [Egypt's Pubs] (Cairo: Rawafid, 2016).

Kırlı, Cengiz, 'Coffeehouses: Public Opinion in the Nineteenth Century Ottoman
   Empire', in A. Salvatore and D. F. Eickelman (eds), *Public Islam and the Common
   Good* (Leiden: Brill, 2004), pp. 75–97.

Kratka, Zuzana, 'A View from the Banks of the Nile', *Banipal* 27 (Autumn/Winter,
   2006). Available at http://www.banipal.co.uk/book_reviews/22/zuzana-kratka-
   reviews-two-novels-by-ibrahim-aslan/ (accessed 1 February 2018).

Lane, Edward W., *An Account of the Manners and Customs of the Modern Egyptians*
   (London: John Murray, 1860).

Lefebvre, Henri, *The Production of Space*, D. Nicolson-Smith (trans.) (Oxford: Basil
   Blackwell, 1991).

LeGassick, Trevor, 'Mahfuz's *al-Karnak*: The Quiet Conscience of Nasir's Egypt
   Revealed', *Middle East Journal* 31/2 (Spring 1977), pp. 205–12.

Lyons, Malcolm, C., *The Arabian Folk Epic: Heroic and Oral Story-Telling, Volume
   One: Introduction* (Cambridge: Cambridge University Press, 1995).

Lewicka, Paulina B., *Food and Foodways of Medieval Cairenes: Aspects of Life in an
   Islamic Metropolis of the Eastern Mediterranean* (Leiden: Brill, 2011).

Mahfouz, Naguib, *Al Karnak* (Cairo: Dar al-Shorouk, 2015).

Mahfouz, Naguib, *Al Sukkariyya* (Cairo: Dar al-Shorouk, 2015).

Mahfouz, Naguib, *Al Summan wal Kharif* (Cairo: Dar al-Shorouk, 2003).

Mahfouz, Naguib, *Autumn Quail*, R. Allen (trans.) (Cairo: American University in
   Cairo Press, 1985).

Mahfouz, Naguib, *The Coffeehouse*, R. Stock (trans.) (Cairo: American University in
   Cairo Press, 2010).

Mahfouz, Naguib, *The Harafish*, C. Cobham (trans.) (New York: Anchor
   Books, 1995).

Mahfouz, Naguib, *Karnak Café*, R. Allen (trans.) (Cairo: American University in
   Cairo Press, 2007).

Mahfouz, Naguib, *Khan Al-Khalili*, R. Allen (trans.) (New York: Anchor
   Books, 2008).

Mahfouz, Naguib, *Khan al-Khalili* (Cairo: Dar al-Shorouk, 2014).

Mahfouz, Naguib, *Midaq Alley*, T. LeGassick (trans.) (Cairo: American University in Cairo Press, 1966).

Mahfouz, Naguib, *Qushtumur* (Cairo: Dar al-Shorouk, 2006).

Mahfouz, Naguib, *Sugar Street*, W. M. Hutchins and A. B. Samaan (trans.) (London: Black Swan, 1994).

Mahfouz, Naguib, *Zoqaq al-Madaq* (Cairo: Dar al-Shorouk, 2014).

Matar Literary Forum (May 2011). Available at http://www.matarmatar.net/threads/34371/ (Arabic) (accessed 28 January 2018).

Mehrez, Samia (ed.), *Translating Egypt's Revolution: The Language of Tahrir* (Cairo: American University in Cairo Press, 2012).

Mitchell, W. J. T., 'Image, Space, Revolution: The Arts of Occupation', *Critical Inquiry* 39/1 (2012), pp. 8–32.

Mourad, Ahmed, *1919* (Cairo: Dar al-Shorouk, 2014).

Mubarak, Salma, *Al Nass wal Soura: Al Cinema wal Adab fi Multaqa al-Turuq* [The Text and the Image: Meeting Points between Cinema and Literature] (Cairo: General Egyptian Book Organisation, 2016).

Nagati, Omar, and Stryker, Beth, *Archiving the City in Flux: Cairo's Shifting Urban Landscape since the January 25th Revolution* (Cairo: CLUSTER, 2013).

al-Nahhas, Hashim, *Salah Abu Seif: Mohawarat Hashim al-Nahhas* [Salah Abu Seif: Conversations with Hashim al-Nahhas] (Cairo: General Egyptian Book Organisation, 1996).

Oakes, Steve, and Warnaby, Gary, 'Conceptualizing the Management and Consumption of Live Music in Urban Space', *Marketing Theory* 11/4 (2011), pp. 405–18.

Osman, Tarek, 'Stirring Up a Revolution', *BBC Radio 3* (9 June 2013). Available at http://www.bbc.co.uk/programmes/b02626dc (accessed 20 June 2019).

Ouyang, Win-chin, 'Naguib Mahfouz', *Literary Encyclopedia online* (5 May 2011). Available at https://www.litencyc.com/php/speople.php?rec=true&UID=12076 (accessed 1 February 2018).

Peterson, Mark A., *Connected in Cairo: Growing up Cosmopolitan in the Modern Middle East* (Bloomington: Indiana University Press, 2011).

Posey, Jacquie, 'Dissertation on Early 20th-Century Cairo Coffeehouses Leads Penn PhD Student to Egyptian and British Spy Reports' (19 June 2017). Available at https://news.upenn.edu/news/dissertation-early-20th-century-cairo-coffeehouses-leads-penn-phd-student-egyptian-and-british (accessed 22 June 2017).

Rafeq, Abdul-Karim, 'The Socioeconomic and Political Implications of the Introduction of Coffee into Syria, 16th–18th Centuries', in M. Tuchscherer (ed.), *Le commerce du café: Avant l'ère des plantations colonials, Cahier des annals islamologiques 20–2001* (Cairo: Institut Français d'Archéologie Orientale, 2001), pp. 127–42.

Raymond, Andre, *Al Hirafiyyun wa al-tujjar fi al-Qahira fi al-qarn al-thamin 'ashr (Artisans et commerçants au Caire au XVIIIe siècle)*, N. Ibrahim and B. Jamaluddin (trans.) (Cairo: al-Majlis al-'Ala lil-Thaqafa, 2005), pp. 174–80.

Reynolds, Dwight, F., *Arab Folklore: A Handbook* (Westport, CT: Greenwood Press, 2007).

al-Sa'dani, Mahmoud, *Hikayat Qahwet Katkut* [The Tales of Katkut Café] (Cairo: Dar al-Shorouq, 2010).

Sajdi, Dana, *The Barber of Damascus: Nouveau Literacy in the Eighteenth-Century Ottoman Levant* (Stanford, CA: Stanford University Press, 2013).

Shafik, Viola, *Arab Cinema: History and Cultural Identity* (Cairo: American University in Cairo Press, 2007).

Shafik, Viola, *Popular Egyptian Cinema: Gender, Class, and Nation* (Cairo: American University in Cairo Press, 2007).

Shemeis, Abdel Mon'eim, *Qahawi al-Adab wal Fann fil Qahira* [The Coffeehouses of Literature and Art in Cairo] (Cairo: Dar al-Ma'arif, 1991).

Sims, David, *Understanding Cairo: The Logic of a City out of Control* (Cairo: American University in Cairo Press, 2012).

Spivak, Gayatri C., 'Can the Subaltern Speak?', in P. Williams and L. Chrisman (eds), *Colonial Discourse and Postcolonial Theory: A Reader* (New York: Columbia University Press, 1993), pp. 66–111.

Straw, Will, 'Systems of Articulation, Logic of Change: Communities and Scenes in Popular Music', *Cultural Studies* 5/3 (1991), pp. 368–88.

Tietze, Andreas, *Mustafa Ali's Description of Cairo of 1599, Text, Transliteration, Translation, Notes* (Vienna: Verlag der Österreichischen Akademie der Wissenschaften, 1975).

Tjora, Aksel, and Scambler, Graham (eds), *Café Society* (New York: Palgrave Macmillan, 2013).

Tripp, Charles, *The Power and the People: Paths of Resistance in the Middle East* (Cambridge: Cambridge University Press, 2013).

'Urghul Bayram al-Tounsi' (Poems of Bayram al-Tounsi), *Al Ahram* newspaper (4 October 2014).

Williams, James, *Space and Being in Contemporary French Cinema* (Manchester: Manchester University Press, 2013).

Feature and Documentary Films

Abdel Khaliq, Ali (dir.), *Garei al-Wuhoush* [Race of the Beasts] (Egypt: Hussein al-Sabbah Films, 1987).

Abdel Sayyed, Daoud (dir.), *Al Kitkat* [Kitkat] (Egypt: Al Alamiyya for TV and Cinema – Hussein Kalla, 1991).

Abul Nasr, Hisham (dir.), *Qahwet el Mawardi* [Mawardi Café] (Egypt: Hisham Abul Nasr Films, 1981).

Abu Seif, Salah (dir.), *Al Saqqa Mat* [The Water Carrier Is Dead] (Egypt: Misr International Film Company; Tunisia: Tunisian Company for Cinematic Development and Production, 1977).

Abu Shadi, Saly (dir.), 'Café Riche', Al Jazeera Documentary Channel (2 July 2015). Available at https://www.youtube.com/watch?v=HNNmcSuUnhw&frags=pl%2Cwn (accessed 30 August 2018).

Abu Zikri, Kamla (dir.), *Malik wi Ketaba* [Heads & Tails] (Egypt: Al Batriq Company for Artistic Production, 2006).

Badrakhan, Ali (dir.), *Al Gou'* [Hunger] (Egypt: Egypt Video Cassette, 1986).

Badrakhan, Ali (dir.), *Al Karnak* (Egypt: Leithi Films, 1975).

Bishara, Khayri (dir.), *Youm Morr, Youm Helw* [Sour Day, Good Day] (Egypt: Al Alamiyya for TV and Cinema – Hussein Kalla, 1988).

Fawzi, Hussein (dir.), *Baladi wi Khiffa* [Traditional and Sweet] (Egypt: Nahhas Films, 1950).

Hilal, Sherif (dir.), 'Sayyed Darwish Café', Al Jazeera Documentary Channel (29 June 2015). Available at https://www.youtube.com/watch?v=SxTRIgwdHg0&frags=pl%2Cwn (accessed 8 February 2019).

Hilal, Sherif (dir.), 'Borset al-Fallah Café', Al Jazeera Documentary Channel (1 July 2015). Available at https://www.youtube.com/watch?v=iIg_WBW71zs&frags=pl%2Cwn (accessed 30 August 2018).

al-Imam, Hassan (dir.), *Al Sukarriyya* [Sugar Street] (Egypt: Sobhi Farahat Films, 1973).

al-Imam, Hassan (dir.), *Qasr al-Shouq* [Palace of Desire] (Egypt: Helmi Rafla Films, 1967).

al-Imam, Hassan (dir.), *Zoqaq al-Madaq* [Midaq Alley] (Egypt: Ramsis Naguib Films – Arab Company for Cinema, 1963).

al-Kashif, Radwan (dir.), *L eih ya Banafseg* [Violet Flowers, Why?] (Egypt: Dana for Artistic Production and Distribution, 1993).

Lotfi, Arab (dir.), *Saba' Layali wi Subhiyya* [Seven Nights and a Dawn] (Egypt: Satellite Specialised Nile Channels, 1998).

Mustapha, Hossam Elddin (dir.), *Al Harafish* [The Harafish] (Egypt: Mohammed Fawzi Films, 1986).

Mustapha, Niazi (dir.), *Al Tout wal Nabbout* (The Mulberry and the Club) (Egypt: Guirguis Fawzi Films, 1986).

'Qahwet Ba'ra', Al Nahar TV Channel (22 January 2017). Available at https://www.youtube.com/watch?v=sItUgM0qiYs (accessed 24 August 2018).

Salem, Atef (dir.), *Khan al-Khalili* (Egypt: General Egyptian Cinema Organisation, 1967).

Selim, Kamal (dir.), *Al 'Azeema* [Determination] (Egypt: Studio Misr, 1939).

Shafiq, Amgad (dir.), 'Zahrat al-Bustan café', Al Jazeera Documentary Channel (14 July 2015). Available at https://www.youtube.com/watch?v=eV6zsFykj90&frags=pl%2Cwn (accessed 10 February 2019).

al-Telmissany, Kamel (dir.), *A l Souq al-Sowda* [Black Market] (Egypt: Misr Company for Acting and Cinema, 1945).

Zulfuqar, Ezz Elddin (dir.), *Sharei' al-Hobb* [Love Street] (Egypt: Helmi Rafla Films, 1958).

Songs

Ali, Islam, 'Qahwa baladi' ['Café], 2014. Available at http://www.youtube.com/watch?v=vtnPQM0CYu0#t=250 (accessed 15 April 2019).

Asmahan, 'Ana Ahwa' ['I am in Love'], 1944. Available at https://www.youtube.com/watch?v=oqh60M05Vmo&frags=pl%2Cwn (accessed 20 January 2018).

al-Gizawi, Omar, 'Itfaddal gahwa' ['Please come in and have some coffee'], n.d. Available at https://www.youtube.com/watch?v=hDWxOF9vF_o&frags=pl%2Cwn (accessed 20 January 2018).

Haidy, 'Ahwa baladi' ['Café/I love my country'], 2011. Available at http://www.youtube.com/watch?v=wohkVPre5Vc (accessed 15 April 2019).

Munib, Ahmed, 'Talab al-ahwa wi ma shribhash' ['He asked for coffee and didn't drink it'], n.d. Available at https://www.youtube.com/watch?v=bIa_gfffJmk&frags=pl%2Cwn (accessed 20 January 2018).

Namira, Hamza, '3alAahwa' ['At the café'], 2012. *Nogoum FM*. Available at http://www.youtube.com/watch?v=dpCLPSfAcNI (accessed 15 April 2019).

Index

Plate 1 A view of Café Riche from outside

Plate 2 A view from inside al-Horriyya Coffeehouse and Bar

Plate 3 A view from the spacious back garden of Le Grillon Coffeehouse and Bar

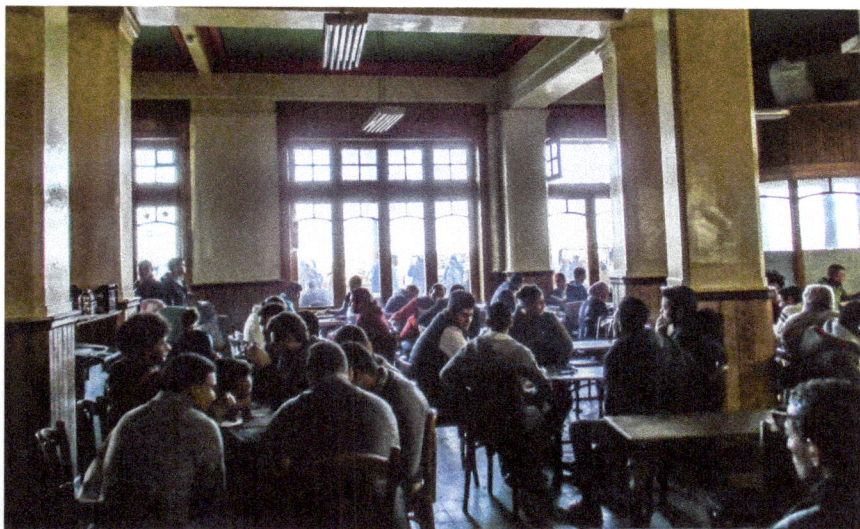

Plate 4 A view (indoors) of al-Borsa al-Tigariyya Café

Plate 5 A view from outside Trianon Coffeehouse opening onto the square